National Service – An Insider's Story

25. Dec 2006

M.J DICKENSON, (1917 1188)
LYPIATT LODGE
LYPIATT
STROUD
GLOS
GL6 7LJ

Given to Dad by Keith for Christmas

Very Best Wishes

E. G. Barraclough

National Service
An Insider's Story

E.G. Barraclough

Pentland Books
Edinburgh – Cambridge – Durham – USA

Contents

	List of Illustrations	vii
	Foreword	ix
	Preface	xi
Chapter I	Did You Do National Service? I Did	1
Chapter II	Showers of Shit in Shropshire	3
Chapter III	Issue of Equipment and Bedspace	5
Chapter IV	The Blanco Fiasco	8
Chapter V	My Prick is a Screwdriver	10
Chapter VI	Thieves Among the NCOs	14
Chapter VII	Goodbye to Oswestry	17
Chapter VIII	The Introduction to Carter Barracks at Bulford on Salisbury Plain	20
Chapter IX	Kill the Enemy at All Times	23
Chapter X	Charlie's Great Blunder	27
Chapter XI	Guard Duties	31
Chapter XII	Sick Parade and the Crabs	34
Chapter XIII	Learning to be a Signaller	37
Chapter XIV	The Firing Ranges at Tidworth and More Infantry Training	40
Chapter XV	Ghosties, Ghoulies, Wee Willie Winkies and Things That Move in the Night	43
Chapter XVI	The Battle of Weybourne	46
Chapter XVII	The Underground Shelter, Dumbelle Wood and the Cricket Pavilion	52
Chapter XVIII	Hello Hobbs Barracks	55

Chapter XIX   More of the Carryings On at Hobbs   60

Chapter XX   The Firing Camp at Sennybridge   64

Chapter XXI   Hobbs Barracks and More of the Happenings   67

Chapter XXII   The Manoeuvres at Lingfield – The Coal Detail –
Lingfield Bonfire Night and Other Events   70

Chapter XXIII   New Officer in Signals Team – The Antics of a
Cab-happy Officer – A Day to be Proud of
During My Service   72

Chapter XXIV   Throw Their Kit Out of the Window   77

Chapter XXV   Firing Camp at Towen – Richard Dimbleby's
Visit   79

Chapter XXVI   The Assault Course at Hobbs Barracks   84

Chapter XXVII   The Raid on the Armoury – Women with the
.303 Rifle — More Happenings at
Hobbs Barracks   88

Chapter XXVIII   My Very Last Guard Duty – Getting near
to Demob   95

Chapter XXIX   The Last Few Days at Hobbs   98

Illustrations

The Author at age 18   11

Gnr Barraclough, Jones, Edwards and Arkell   24

Outside the cookhouse tent at Weybourne   47

Beans and Chips supper in Naafi   49

This could be the last pillbox at Weybourne   50

L/Bdr Douglas Gordon Goody   52

Just been swimming in Cardigan Bay   81

Bombadier Barraclough   85

German 88mm   99

British 3.7mm   99

Foreword

IT GIVES ME ENORMOUS PLEASURE to write a short foreword to this book, *National Service – An Insider's Story.*

As a young boy growing up in Yorkshire throughout the 1950s I used to enjoy visiting my grandmother and would be particularly delighted if one of my uncles happened to be home on leave from the army. They would tell fascinating stories from far off exotic places, Catterick, Aldershot and Longmoor and they would repeat the tales with great enthusiasm and a little more detail each time told. All men joined the army, or so I thought, some of course the RAF but it was the Army for me. I longed for the time when I would be old enough, I wanted some of the excitement, the daring, the thrills, the shiny boots and a penknife with a corkscrew and a tin opener. I wanted to do what these heroes did, to talk about sergeants, sergeant majors and officers, to have a 48-hour pass and to go to a Naafi, to do rifle drill, to march, to be on guard duty, to be on parade, to be put on a charge or to go AWOL. One day soon it would be my turn but then conscription stopped, a word I had heard so much about and become so familiar with.

What fabulous times these soldiers and airmen had, memories forever, remembering the good times, forgetting the bad. The marvellous friends, the camaraderie, the banter, the laughter. These were the days when the general public travelled very little, Taffs, Jocks, Geordies, Brummies and Scousers, accents never heard before. These were young men often away from home for the first time, total strangers assembled together for basic training in soldiering, but more importantly life.

This book is written by my uncle; he was one of the large family who told me so much about army life. He remembers with astonishing detail the amazing events of his National Service days, the hilarious escapades and the characters of which there are so many. Everyone who reads this book will remember similar events, will have their own stories and will remember with fondest memories their time as a National Serviceman. For anyone who was not called upon to complete National Service, this is what you missed.

I did in the end join the Army, probably as a result of all the tales told as a young boy, it was an enormous influence on my life. During a very gratifying career I also met the same sort of characters. Army life was every bit as I expected it to be and how it had been described to me; these people that I had heard so much about were actually real. I completed 26 years in total joining as a private soldier and retiring as a commissioned officer in 1998.

Some ex-National Servicemen were still in the Army when I joined. They were the ones who were coming towards the end of their long careers and who had done what all National Servicemen had said since: "I wish that I had stayed in".

Gwyn Barraclough
Captain (Retd) G. G. Barraclough
Royal Electrical and Mechanical Engineers
Royal Corps of Transport
Royal Logistic Corps

Preface

THESE WRITINGS ARE OF MY NATIONAL SERVICE; some of the events are imprinted in my mind never to be forgotten; some of the events may not have happened in the order they are recorded; some of the people involved may have forgotten.

Many people will say that National Service was a waste of time. It was not. National Service taught young men discipline and respect, respect for other people, their property and belongings. It taught teamwork and comradeship. Yes there were 'bully boys' amongst the NCOs, but not all of them. Some were humane. To many young men who had never been in a cadet force, it would have been very hard when NCOs were screaming and using foul language at them.

Having got over the first three months of army training it would not bother them any more. There were young men who would never have got used to army life. The Government should have compensated families who had lost wage earners. There were the young men who kicked against authority because they were there through no fault of their own; many served time in Military Detention Barracks where the regime was full of 'bully boys' and everything they did was at the double.

Most of us were continually skint (hard up), waiting from one pay day to the next. The military prisons were and still are ten times worse then civilian prisons. I wonder if the pawn shop (no, not porn shop) in East Grindstead is still there where many young men pawned their watches, and never had enough money to redeem them before leaving the Army.

I may have been harsh about some of the NCOs and the way they treated new recruits but that was how I saw them. One thing about the Army was they wouldn't give you the sack, and you couldn't give them a week's notice.

What would happen in this day and age if you were called names like you were called in the 1940s and 1950s?

NCOs would on many occasions show you up in front of your mates if you did anything wrong.

'You are a fucking Nig Nog, lad. What are you?' And they would make the recruit repeat it.

They would call you Coons?/Idiots/stupid cunts and any other name they could think of, but we had a stringent rule about not being called a bastard. Most of them would not dare to call you that, many would refer to the whole lot of us as 'stupid bastards' but they dare not call an individual one. I made a promise that I would never treat men like animals if I ever made promotion. I also promised myself that I would never put anyone under my authority on a charge (252), but unfortunately I had it forced upon me to put two lads on a charge.

Two other lads had lost their blanco brushes and reported to the troop officer that they had gone missing. Some hours later two lads came to me with the brushes and said they had found them in the blanco room, so although the blanco room had been searched I gave these two lads the benefit of the doubt. I told the troop officer that the brushes had been found and said where they were found and by whom, and was ordered to put them on a charge. 'What for?' I asked. 'Stealing by finding,' said the officer. 'We won't tolerate it.'

Although I explained to the Battery Commander and spoke up for these lads, they both got seven days CB (mounting with the guard). Bang went my record of never putting anyone on a charge.

You have been out of the Army for nearly fifty years.

You have never seen any of the lads that you were in with since. How many names of them can you remember?

Lt. Col. Bannerman DSO, reputed at that time to be the youngest colonel in the Army.

Major Bailward	Lt Ross	
Captain Ball	Sgt Russell	Gnr Feaks
Captain Davis	Sgt Williams	Gnr Greenaway
Lt Chappel	Sgt Wingate	Gnr Tubb
Lt Claydon	Sgt Brittain	Gnr Whiting
Lt Perret Young	Sgt Bayliss	Gnr McMurray
Captain Start	Sgt Liley	Gnr Marlowe
RSM Boldock	Sgt Price	Gnr Griffin
BSM Stamp	Sgt Ramshaw	Gnr Shears
Bdr Gillespie	Gnr Bradford	Gnr Shone
Bdr O'Connel	Bdr Nicholls	Bdr Harris
Bdr Haylott	Gnr Wood	Gnr Carrol
Bdr Allen	Gnr Jenkins	Gnr Neary
Bdr Musgrave	Gnr Jones, Wigan	Gnr Griffiths
Bdr Head	Gnr Jones, Wales	Gnr Huttley
Bdr Adams	Gnr Arkel	Gnr Songhurst
Gnr McLean	Gnr Bestwick	Gnr Gladys
Gnr Burgess	Gnr Evens	Gnr York
Gnr Foots	Gnr Edwards 442	Gnr Smith
Gnr Rhodes X Troop	Gnr Edwards	Gnr McLennon
Gnr Ashley X Troop	Gnr Payne	Gnr Mclellan
Gnr Tomlinson	Gnr Pow	Gnr McKinnon
CSM Mallard WRAC	Gnr Hole	Gnr Raffle
Sgt Scott WRAC	Gnr Clegg	Gnr Bruce
Lt Dene WRAC	Gnr Weeks	Gnr Glover
Lt Carter WRAC	Gnr Marwood	Gnr Miles
Sgt Williams AEC (WRAC)	Gnr Goody	Gnr Smullen
Pte Armitage WRAC	Gnr Delaney	Gnr Hood
Pte Nicholls WRAC	Gnr Livingstone	Gnr Wilson (Tug)
Pte McCracken WRAC	Gnr Ayres, X Troop	Bdr Berry
Pte Curry WRAC	Gnr Parkin, X Troop	Gnr Harker
Pte Gerrish WRAC	Gnr McMurray	Gnr Hannon
Pte Aitkinhead WRAC	Pte Pratton WRAC	Sgt Finney
Gnr Cairns	Pte Swan WRAC	Sgt Rogers

Ginger Connie from Leeds WRAC	Cpl Tuck WRAC	Gnr Fellows
Jean from Leeds WRAC	Bdr Musgrave's girlfriend	Gnr Wright
Gnr McNiven	Gnr McNinnen	Gnr Charlie Bonner

I have remembered all these names; all whose names I haven't remembered are there in my mind's eye, faces that I can't put a name to, but I still remember you.

Chapter I

Did You Do National Service? I Did.

National Service Acts Certification of Registration Occ. Class No.
LL5407. Registration No. BFP 55719
Holder's name: Eric George Barraclough, 7, Bolland Buildings, Low
Moor, Bradford, West Yorkshire. 21/6/1950

I WAS CALLED TO ATTEND A MEDICAL EXAMINATION at the Mechanics
Institute, Bradford on 21 June 1950 to assess my fitness for military service.
There was no doubt in my mind that I would be passed A1 fit (A. One).
Three of my elder brothers had served throughout the War, and a fourth
brother was doing his national service in Egypt at this time.

My father had a very good sense of humour, even though it was a very
crude one, and I was given a lecture before I went off for my medical.

'They will tell you to bend over and then shine a torch up your backside,'
said my father.

'Why will they do that?' I asked.

'To see if you hat is on straight,' replied my father. 'They will then ask
you what is Rule 55,' said my father.

'What is Rule 55?' I asked.

'Never let them dangle,' said my father.

'Never let what dangle?' I asked.

'Your braces,' said my father. 'Pretend to be deaf,' he said, 'but don't
let them catch you out. As you walk out they will call you to shut the
door; don't shut it.'

I was always getting in trouble at school for sniggering at anything that
I thought was funny; here I was again at my medical sniggering at all the
things I was tickled by. Not only was I sniggering and trying to conceal
it, but I had started a lot more of the young men who were awaiting their
turn for examination.

'Drop you pants and cough,' said one doctor. I couldn't help but laugh.
'Pass some urine into this test tube,' said another doctor. I got into trouble
for continually laughing and making all the others laugh.

1

I was working in a Jute mill at the time. I had also been a member of the local Army Cadets from the age of thirteen, having given the wrong age – I should have been fourteen.

At the age of fourteen I must have been very naive, one of three males working with ten females. When overtime was offered, there was just myself and one woman who would work over; while we were working over a man from the local railway depot would come and visit us. 'Go and drive my lorry around the yard but don't go out onto the road,' he would say to me. It was a very big yard called the 'New Biggin Yard' and I was delighted to be able to drive around. The lorry was a three-wheeler Scammel cob, known as a six-ton mechanical horse, and through trial and error I soon became a competent driver.

I started going out on the roads with the lorry and would pick up many of my friends, taking them on trips around Low Moor and Wyke villages (showing off I suppose). People would stare at us, and I suppose they would think that I looked too young to drive.

When the driver found out that I had been on the main roads, he gave me a hiding and told me I wouldn't be driving his lorry any more, but next time we were working over he let me drive again (to get me out of the mill), but not to go out of the yard.

I was asked at the medical what regiment I would like to go into and told them that I would like to be in the RASC (Royal Army Service Corps) because I wanted to become a vehicle driver.

Chapter II

Showers of Shit in Shropshire

HAVING PASSED MY MEDICAL A1, my call-up papers duly arrived. I hadn't been assigned to the RASC but I had managed the first two letters, RA (Royal Artillery). I had to report to the Royal Artillery training camp, 'Park Hall Camp' Oswestry, on 31 July 1950.

I travelled from Low Moor to Manchester Central, and then walked to Manchester London Road station, where I was informed I would change trains at Whitchurch for Oswestry. It was a very hot day and I was very thirsty but I couldn't afford to buy cold drinks. Most working-class families were very poor in the 1950s and I knew what money I had would have to last to my first pay day (whenever that would be).

Hundreds of young men were travelling that day to their respective training camps, you had to go into the Army whether you liked it or not. Many families were losing a wage earner; many families would be a lot poorer for this, but it didn't worry the government.

I arrived at the station in Oswestry in the early afternoon along with many other young men; none of us knew what we were in for but having been in the Army Cadets I wasn't unduly worried. NCOs were on the station platform – bombardiers (corporals), lance bombardiers (lance corporals) and sergeants, screaming at us to get into line.

What a welcome! Quite a number of lads had been in the Army Cadets and were used to being shouted at; others were flinching at the tirade of foul language.

After a few minutes we were herded into three ranks, a sergeant stood in front of us and gave the following speech which I have never forgotten.

'I am Sergeant Eyles [Hiles?]. I am a pure unadulterated bastard, never again in your lives will you ever meet another bastard like me. I have never in my life seen a bigger shower of shit than you lot. Talk about showers of shit in Shropshire, you might have broken you mother's heart, but you won't break mine.'

Here I was again, sniggering and trying my best to stifle it but couldn't.

'Hey you,' screamed Sergeant Eyles, looking straight at me.

3

'Me, sergeant?' I asked.

'Yes you, you fucking baboon, what are you grinning at?'

'I wasn't grinning, I was squinting because the sun is in my eyes,' I said.

'What is your name, laaaaaaaad?' the Sergeant asked.

'Barraclough,' I replied.

The name Barraclough seemed to inflame him. 'Barraclough – Barraclough – Barraclough,' he screamed, 'where do you come from?'

'Bradford,' I replied.

'Yes, I thought so,' said the Sergeant Eyles, 'what relation are you to Roy Barraclough?'

'I don't know anyone called Roy Barraclough,' I replied.

'Fucking liar,' he screamed at me, 'Roy Barraclough came from Bradford, a place called Oakenshaw,' he said. 'He was supposed to be an actor but I called him a Piss artist. He was in the last intake and continually tried to take the piss out of me, now I will get my revenge on one of his relatives. You will suffer for the next six weeks,' he said.

Although the place called Oakenshaw was only about a mile from where I lived, I didn't know Roy Barraclough, and I told the Sergeant that there were hundreds of Barracloughs in Bradford and they were not all related.

The Sergeant kept on about Roy Barraclough taking the piss out of him, then a voice from the ranks said, 'You can't take the piss out a pile of shit like you.' No one would own up to having said it, but as we boarded the lorries to take us to the training camp a young lad with a Liverpool accent said to me, 'It looks like you are in for a rough time here.'

This lad was overhead talking to me, and the Sergeant screamed and shouted at him for talking and asked him his name.

'Smullen,' said the lad, 'My name is Ted Smullen.'

'Well,' said the Sergeant, 'you will join Barraclough on my list of undesirable characters.'

'Couldn't give a fuck,' replied Ted Smullen.

We arrived at the training camp and NCOs were shouting and bawling, using foul language at us. You would have thought that some of the little lance bombardiers (one stripe) were generals, but they were nothing but jumped up little Adolph Hitlers who were letting the little bit of authority go to their heads.

It was clear to see that many of the NCOs were in a gang of their own; they must have forgotten that they had been new recruits at some time.

Chapter III

Issue of Equipment and Bedspace

A LL THE NEW INTAKE WERE PARADED from the lorries then marched in single file into what was known as a 'Barrack Spider', wooden huts with eight rooms and ablutions. Twenty men to each room, we were allocated one steel wardrobe, one iron bed, one foot locker for small items of kit.

We were then marched to the QM stores (Quartermaster's Stores), a very long building with a large noticeboard on the side where you entered; this board told you:

YOU ARE ABOUT TO BE ISSUED WITH TWENTY POUNDS WORTH OF GOV-
ERNMENT PROPERTY. IF YOU LOSE ANY OF THIS PROPERTY YOU WILL
PAY FOR IT. YOU WILL ALSO PAY FOR THE REPLACEMENT ITEM THAT IS
ISSUED, SO BEWARE.

One lad shouted that was the reason that a captain went down with his ship so that he didn't have to pay for two, adding that he hoped they didn't issue him with a field gun.

Sergeant Eyles wasn't amused and put this lad on his hit list; his name should have been Sergeant Evil.

We were issued with two of everything in clothing and one of everything in webbing except gaiters, of which we did get two pairs. As you went down the inside of the building there were counters with a storeman stood behind; as you came to each counter the storeman would take a look at you and shout what he thought were your measurements; his assistant would then throw an item of equipment at you for which you signed and moved on to the next counter.

Eventually you came out at the other end of the building loaded down with kit plus a pint pot; many of the lads dropped the pint pot and had to pay for another two.

We all staggered back to the barrack rooms and dropped all the kit onto our beds; we were then called outside again and marched to the regimental barber for our first army haircut.

The first haircut in the Army was supposed to be free, but ours wasn't because the NCOs had a scam going. The barber put his shears to the back of your head and shaved straight over until you were cropped nearly bald.

As you left the barber's shop the NCOs stood at each side of the door and demanded one shilling, which in 1950 was a lot of money to us people who came from poor families. Some of the lads whose hair was their pride and joy actually started crying when they saw themselves in the mirror.

We were issued with stencils with which to mark our army number on clothing. We also had metal stamps with which to stamp our number on the uppers of boots and identity discs; the housewife issued was a small cotton bag with needles and cotton/darning wool for sewing jobs. Buttons were issued for sewing onto the army greatcoat, although most of the lads had never had to use needles and cotton in their lives.

All the ex-army cadets knew what it was all about, as we had experienced in marching, cleaning kit, use of weapons; many had passed Certificate 'A' parts one and two, which required you to have fired a Bren gun/rifle, thrown a grenade and depending on what cadet force you had been in (infantry or artillery), other skills like mortar/PIAT (Personnel Infantry Anti Tank), Bangalore Torpedo etc., but we were in the minority.

I would go so far as to say that many of the ex-cadets were more experienced than the jumped-up little Hitlers who would be responsible for our training. It was plain to see who the experienced sergeants were by their campaign ribbons from the War. Most of the ex-cadets had brought their own cleaning materials with them, i.e. brasso/blanco/boot polish/dusters.

Here was another scam by the NCOs: they had gone to the NAAFI (Navy Army Air Force Institute) Canteen and bought up all supplies of cleaning materials which they knew would be needed by the new intake. Then they came around the barrack rooms selling the cleaning materials at very inflated prices, but were not amused when the ex-cadets didn't buy anything from them. Those who had to buy and couldn't pay there and then were entered as owing in a notebook until the first pay day.

It had now got to seven o'clock in the evening when one lad shouted out that if he didn't get fed soon he would faint, so someone decided to march us to the cookhouse for a meal. The meal wasn't too bad except for the split peas and lentils; I had never eaten split peas and lentils in my life and I wasn't going to start now.

When everyone had returned to the barracks, we were told to blanco all our kit and get all brasses shone up ready for parade next morning. One lad asked the NCOs what he meant by blanco all your kit; the NCO replied that he and all his gang were going to the NAAFI for their usual nightly booze-up (probably paid for out of their ill-gotten gains) and that he would leave it to the ex-army cadets to show all the others what blancoing was all about.

Khaki Green 103, Royal Artillery colour – the block of blanco was three inches in diameter and one and a half inches thick, a solid block of green chalk.

We went into the blanco room and I demonstrated my way – wet the blanco brush (like a nail brush), rub the brush over the webbing (belt/gaiters/ammo packs etc.) then rub the block of blanco onto the webbing and smooth it out with the wet brush.

Another cadet showed how he blancoed by wetting his brush, rubbing it onto the blanco and smoothing it onto his webbing.

We then demonstrated the use of the button stick, and how to avoid getting brasso on clothing and webbing; if anyone had seen us it would have been thought that the ex-cadets were the instructors.

Chapter IV

The Blanco Fiasco

ALL TROOPS WERE OUT ON PARADE AT 0600 HOURS (6.00 a.m.), everyone seemed to have made a good effort at getting their kit reasonably clean it would be many weeks before the brasses and the boots would shine like glass; (the word for getting boots and brasses really shiny was 'bullshit') and there were many different ways of bulling boot heels; ex-soldiers will no doubt know these methods including the electric iron.

Our troop officer was introduced to us for the first time on this early morning parade. The troop was called to attention, open order marched and the officer began his inspection of the first rank of men.

We in the first rank couldn't see what was going on in the rear rank, but we heard the officer shout in a very posh voice, 'Oh facking hell, where are you clothes, lad?'

We then heard the reply, 'I've blancoed them, sir.'

'What do you mean you've blancoed them? Are you facking mad?'

'No sir, I was told to blanco all my kit so I've nothing to wear' (we had been issued with brown paper and string to send our civvy clothes home) and these were now in the QM stores ready for despatch.

'Tell me the whole story,' said the officer.

'Well sir, I asked the NCOs to show me what to do, they replied that they were going to the NAAFI for their nightly booze-up and that the ex-army cadets would have to show us; some of them did show us their methods but I invented my own way which was much easier.'

'What did you do?' asked the officer.

'Well sir, I crushed up my block of blanco into a powder, I then filled one of the big pot sinks with cold water and stirred in the powder. This made a nice khaki solution just like a dye; I then dipped all my kit into it steel helmet and all.'

'Do you mean to tell me that you dipped your greatcoat and all your underwear?' said the officer.

'Yes sir, and now all my kit is hung out on a line at the back of the billets drying.' The NCOs got a bollocking like they never had in their lives, and the lad in question was given denims to wear and marched off to see the doctor.

The regimental tailor then turned up with his assistants, tape measure and blue chalk. Each man was measured and blue chalk was placed on the uniform where alterations were needed; we then went and changed into our second uniform to be measured and one uniform was taken away to be altered where needed.

Training started straight after breakfast. Sergeant Eyles was in top form shouting his obscenities at anyone who went wrong but concentrating on myself and Ted Smullen. One lad from Goole (excused boots) said he had planned his discharge with his father before coming into the Army. He was wearing shoes with a strip of leather nailed across the instep and said they were surgical shoes (we all thought he was having us on). Some days later he received a parcel from home with two pairs of shoes with a strip of leather nailed across the instep which he showed to the officer.

Training went on

As the training went on I was continually congratulated on my turnout; boots/brasses and uniform were getting to the same standard as my army cadet kit had been. The troop officer questioned some of us as to how we were becoming so efficient in drill and weapon training; we in turn said that the Army Cadets had prepared us for the real Army, and I was no stranger to military affairs as three of my brothers had gone right through the War and one brother was now serving in Egypt.

One of my brothers had won the Military Medal after being badly wounded in Italy; he was taking water and rations up to the front line and at the time saved the life of his officer.

Sergeant Eyles didn't worry me one bit – I knew that he couldn't do anything so long as I kept out of trouble but the language he used was abominable.

Chapter V

My Prick is a Screwdriver

EVERY MORNING WE WOULD BE MARCHED to the barrack square for drill. One morning we were being marched there and Ted Smullen finally broke his silence because of the continual harassment we were getting.

Sergeant Eyles kept shouting, 'Smullen, swing you fucking arms. Smullen get in fucking step. Smullen stop talking' (when he wasn't). 'Barraclough, stop fucking grinning. Barraclough stop trying to take the piss like your relative did. Smullen, you're not swinging your arms.' Suddenly Ted Smullen stepped out from the ranks and started dancing alongside the Sergeant. 'Smullen do this, Smullen do that, Smullen do this. Am I the only fucking man in this troop or is your brain geared on Smullen?' he said.

We all thought that Ted was about to drop one on the Sergeant's chin but he didn't, he just kept on mimicking the Sergeant's voice, 'Smullen do this Smullen, do that.' Two NCOs fell in at each side of Ted, and on the order of Sergeant Eyles he was marched off to the cookhouse to spend the day scrubbing out greasy tins. We arrived on the barrack square and Sergeant Eyles picked on me again, 'Your fucking capbadge is filthy,' he said.

'Can't be, Sergeant, I was complimented on how my capbadge was as shiny at the back as it was at the front,' I said.

'Don't fucking answer me back or you will join that cunt Smullen in the cookhouse,' he said.

'I'm not answering you back, and I suggest that you consult the troop officer as to what he said to me at morning inspection,' I said.

'If you cleaned you badge this morning then my fucking prick is a screwdriver,' he said. He snatched my capbadge from my beret and flung it as far as he could into the long grass surrounding the barrack square.

Now he said, 'You can stay here and look for your badge while the rest of us got for our NAAFI break.' In the meantime I was told to double round the barrack square with a dummy artillery shell (about twenty pounds) above my head.

The Author at age 18, one week into army life at Oswestry – Shropshire.

I had done about ten circuits of the barrack square when they went for their break, and I was then told to find my badge. I had noted the direction in which it was thrown and retrieved it within ten minutes; I was having a smoke when the troop returned and the Sergeant was not very pleased.

In the 1950s cigarette lighters were mostly petrol fed, gas lighters were very rare and one of the lads had bought a tube of petrol during his break intending to fill his lighter. He couldn't get the screw out of the bottom of the lighter, and asked if anyone had a screwdriver, so I told him that Sergeant Eyles had one.

'Excuse me, Sergeant Eyles, can I borrow your screwdriver?' said the lad.

'Now what the fucking hell would I be doing carrying a screwdriver around with me?' said the Sergeant.

'Gunner Barraclough told me that you had one on you,' said the lad.

Sergeant Eyles called me over and asked why I had told this lad that he had a screwdriver.

'It was a joke, Sergeant,' I said.

'Well I don't find it fucking funny, you fucking moron,' said the Sergeant. I explained the joke and told him that earlier on he had said to me that if I had cleaned my badge that morning his prick was a screwdriver, so I sent the lad to borrow it.

He still didn't get the joke and said that I was doing exactly the same as Roy Barraclough (my relative as he called him) taking the piss out of him.

I was then detailed to double round the square with the dummy artillery shell above my head. I had just done three circuits when the troop officer arrived and he must have asked the Sergeant what was going on.

Apparently the Sergeant told him that I was a disruptive influence on the other members of the troop, so the officer came over to me and asked what was I thinking about and said that he thought I was one of the better recruits.

I explained everything to him, which he thought was hilarious and called the Sergeant over. He then told the Sergeant that there had been nothing wrong with my capbadge on morning inspection, in fact he said he had complimented me about my brasses being as shiny at the back as they were at the front.

The officer then brought up the subject of Roy Barraclough because Sergeant Eyles had mentioned him as being a relative. I explained that this was not the case, and that I didn't know Roy Barraclough although he lived about a mile from where I lived.

Sergeant Eyles didn't like it when the officer said that Roy Barraclough was a nice young fellow, and added that he was a fairly decent actor. Ted Smullen and I were being victimised – the Sergeant had taken a dislike to both of us.

After the evening meal I had just started on my kit to get it ready for next morning, when Sergeant Eyles came into the barrack room and detailed me to scrub all the tables in the blanco room, punishment he said for the morning's joke. Ted Smullen had been in the cookhouse all day doing general duties (fatigues), peeling spuds, cleaning tins and pans, but said he had enjoyed it away from 'That Bastard Eyles' (as Ted called him).

Ted thought he had finished, but no, Sergeant Eyles had other ideas, and Ted was detailed to scrub out the whole barrack room. When Sergeant Eyles had gone, everybody in the barrack room got organised, each man scrubbed out his own bedspace and helped with the tables in the blanco room.

The Sergeant expected Ted and myself to be still at it late into the night, but when he called into the barrack room when the NAAFI closed, we were all in bed, kit all ready for the morning inspection.

The young lad from Goole (excused boots), Watson, was discharged as medically unfit, but the lad who had blancoed all his kit didn't manage to work his ticket (as he intended); he had to pay for the kit he ruined and his new issue.

The National Serviceman of the 1950s was treated worse than prisoners in jail, but not by the regular soldiers who had served throughout the War, and before the War. The treatment and bullying was mainly by jumped-up NCOs who had been promoted by greasing and creeping to get a stripe, and I don't mean all NCOs because many had got promoted by hard work and keeping out of trouble.

Chapter VI

Thieves Among the NCOs

WE RETURNED TO OUR BILLET ONE AFTERNOON after a very hard morning's training; all the foot lockers were overturned and everything that had been in them was piled in the middle of the room. Some of the NCOs had been in the billet on the pretext of inspecting the cleanliness of lampshades and windows; they were supposed to have found dust on a lampshade and the punishment was (supposedly) to make the room look like a tip.

After we had sorted out the pile of PT kit underwear, socks etc. it was found that some of us had items of clothing missing, mostly socks and underwear.

We had got to the point where we would be joining our respective regiments in another week; I had already figured out what the reason for the tip was, and I lost no time in voicing my opinion to the NCOs.

Our intake had been issued with the new cellular-type underwear, whereas the NCOs had the old khaki cotton type. How was it possible for many of us to have items missing when all the kit had only been tipped in a pile?

When we complained the NCOs offered us replacements from their own kit, so that we didn't have to pay for two lots, they said, but I wasn't going to wear other people's cast-offs.

When the officer came, I openly accused the NCOs who had tipped everything out of taking the missing clothing. The officer said that a search would be made of their quarters, but I said that it wouldn't make any difference, because the items would be hidden somewhere until out intake had moved out.

Nothing more was done about it and some of us had to buy a set of new underwear and socks and pay for what was missing.

My pay when I was at home had been very good. Working in the rag mill was a dirty job but I was a wage earner and stuck to the job, although I didn't like it.

I came from a family of eleven, including Mother and Father. Since 1939 my mother had lost one wage earner after another which meant that most of the time my father's wage was all that was coming into the home.

It mattered not to the government that families were getting poorer through no fault of their own, but there was no compensation for lost wage earners, in fact it was left to the conscript who had been taken into the Army to try and help his family.

My pay to start with in the Army was twenty-one shillings per week. What was twenty one shillings in 1950 (one hundred and ten pence)? Out of my twenty-one shillings I made an allowance home of seven shillings a week (thirty-five pence now). This was a little help to my parents and Mother drew this from the post office each week by an order book.

Income tax was taken out of the twenty-one shillings – two shillings and six pence (half a crown) or twelve and a half pence now.

There were never any barrack room damages (we wouldn't have dared to do any damage) but every other week we were stopped two shillings or half a crown for barrack room damages. Then the Army expected men to join the post office savings bank, most young men ended up with eight to fourteen shilling a week, depending on whether you had barrack room damages or saved something. Fourteen shillings a week (seventy pence) or eight shillings (forty pence) at today's prices – some lads were better off because they didn't help their families at home. What did a soldier want money for? Razor blades/shaving soap/brasso/boot polish/hair cuts/cigarettes if you were a smoker, and most were, duster/blanco not supplied by the Army. Could you afford to go to the cinema/could you afford beans and chips in the NAAFI? Not very often.

When you had to polish the windows you had to use your own brasso to shine the glass, the stirrup pumps (small hose connected to a pump) had to be blackened with your own boot polish. It was 'Bullshit at it's worst'. Entertainment was NIL unless you had some talent in your troop (piano player or other instruments). This is where I guess that Roy Barraclough had probably been entertaining in the NAAFI.

A few pints of beer were out of the question, but we were lucky to have some very good talent in our battery – Geordie Raffles, brilliant pianist, Charlie Gladys, comedian, not amateur or professional, just very funny. One lad (I don't know his name) was a very good hypnotist. I had never believed in it until I saw the volunteers he got up on the stage to assist him in his act.

15

Sergeant Eyles was there in the audience and kept heckling the act, shouting that they were all faking being hypnotised, so the hypnotist challenged him to take part. If he had not accepted he would have looked a right plonker (he was anyway) so as not to lose face he went up onto the stage.

How good it was to find that he was one of those who succumbed to the state of hypnosis! The hypnotist had him dancing with a brush, having been told it was a beautiful woman, then he was on his hands and knees howling like a dog, then he was lapping water out of a tray.

When he was back to his normal nasty self he was made fun of by some of the young officers but he would not admit that he had been under hypnosis. He said he had been pretending just to entertain the servicemen. He wouldn't live this down for a long time after we had left the place – the officers kept howling as he went past them.

One lad got up on stage and said that he wanted to teach the young conscript officers a song. He thought that all the conscript officers were born with a silver spoon and were from the privileged side of life.

I'll never forget the day I enlisted on the spree
To become a greasy gunner in the Royal Artillery
Oh! how my heart is aching to be in civvy street once more
You ought to see the gunners on a Friday night
Polishing up their brasses in the pale moonlight.
There's going to be an inspection in the morning
And the Battery Sergeant Major will be there, he'll be there,
He'll be there in that little barrack room across the square.
And while we're doing the open order, he'll be shagging the colonel's daughter, in that little barrack room across the square.
Victorious! Victorious! One bottle of beer between four of us.
Glory be to God there isn't any more of us,
Cos one of us could drink the fucking lot … why not?

The officers cheered and shouted for an encore. They wanted to learn the words.

Time was coming near for us to leave this 'Stalag' as we called it; none of us had been out of the camp and even to this day I don't know what the rest of Oswestry is like.

Chapter VII

Goodbye to Oswestry

THE SIX WEEKS OF PRISON LIFE AT OSWESTRY WERE OVER, we were now classed as trained soldiers so far as marching and rifle drill were concerned and much to the annoyance of Sergeant Eyles, I had not let him get me rattled, but more to his annoyance our troop officer had kept commending me on turnout.

Many NCOs had arrived in the camp, sergeants/bombardiers and one officer. We had no idea who they were but we found out when we went for our last breakfast in the camp. The officer was an RTO (Railway Transport Officer); all the other NCOs were there to escort us to our new destination.

We were informed that after breakfast we would get dressed in FSMO (Field Service Marching Order) and parade outside our billets. Lorries were beginning to line up outside, when Sergeant Eyles came to me and gave me a bucket, scrubbing brush and soap. He said he was going to give me something to remember him by.

'Scrub the tables in the blanco room,' he said.

I was dressed in full marching order and told him that the lorries awaited us. 'Fuck the lorries,' he said, 'scrub the tables.'

Then a voice from outside roared out, 'Come on you lucky lads, let's have you aboard these lorries,' I pushed past Sergeant Eyles and made for one of the lorries; his face was rage itself.

A big tall Sergeant was pulling the lads on board, helping them up in all their kit. He had a row of campaign ribbons on his battledress jacket; he also had a very nice Scots accent and it was plain to see that he was one of the humane people in the Army.

We had been issued with haversack rations for our journey: one individual fruit pie, one cheese, one corned beef sandwich, one hard-boiled egg.

We arrived at the station (the only part of Oswestry we had seen) where a special train was waiting for us, although to where we didn't know. Sergeant Eyles and his cronies were on the station as we boarded the train, and they started shouting obscenities at us. One lad suggested that we all throw our hard-boiled eggs at them but one of the sergeants with us said not to do it.

Eventually the train set off and all the lads started shouting obscenities at Sergeant Eyles. One lad shouted, 'Hey Eyles, don't be a cunt all your life, have a day off.'

We were only being shunted out of the sidings and onto the main line, so we had to pass Sergeant Eyles again. There was one lad who was very quiet and had kept himself to himself most of the time, so it was a surprise to us all when we passed Sergeant Eyles for the last time and this lad shouted, 'Sergeant Eyles, I hope that as you slide down the banister of life you get plenty of big splinters in your arse.' We all thought that was a classic.

The NCOs who had come to collect us went up and down the train calling into each compartment and introducing themselves to us, staying a little while to explain where we were going and what we would be doing.

The Scottish sergeant told us he was to be our infantry instructor. Jock Russell was his name and a very pleasant chap he was.

'Where are we going? asked Charlie Gladys.

'Bulford,' said Sergeant Russell.

'Where's that?' said Charlie.

'Right in the middle of Salisbury Plain,' said Sgt Russell.

'I'm no wiser,' said Charlie.

There had been no foul language at all in conversation with Sgt Russell but when Sgt Wingate came and introduced himself the language started flowing. Sgt Wingate was from Leeds and was just as amicable as Sgt Russell, but his sense of humour was like that of Charlie Gladys; he told us that we were going to 'Carter Barracks', and that when we got there we would have to behave ourselves because there were about one hundred members of the WRAC (Women's Royal Army Corps) in the camp because it was a mixed regiment.

Charley Gladys asked if any of the women would do a turn (as he called it). Sgt Wingate said yes, there were some who would do a turn but added that you might have to fight their existing boyfriends.

'Fuck that,' said Charlie, 'I'm not fighting for it. I'm no very good at fighting.'

'You will be when you have been at Bulford for a few months,' said Sgt Wingate.

18

'Why is that?' asked Charlie.

'Because when Sgt Russell takes you for infantry training and he will teach you to fight very dirty,' said Sgt Wingate.

We stopped somewhere along the way (I didn't notice where) but we were served with pint mugs of tea by the WVS (Women's Voluntary Service) – what a fine organisation they were. Once again on our way we met Sgt Brittain, Sgt Ramshaw, Sgt Bayliss and Sgt Williams. They told us that they didn't know yet if we would be in their Batteries or some other.

They told us that we were going to the 46th Heavy Anti-Aircraft Regiment, and that there were three batteries, 117, 124 and 126. Many lads were saying that they would like to be in Sgt Wingate's lot because of his sense of humour; many said they would like to be in Sgt Russell's lot because of his friendliness towards the young lads.

I formed the opinion that Sgt Russell felt sorry for all us young men who had been 'press ganged' into the Army, because it was plain to see that many did not want to be there.

At that time there was a new song by Doris Day, and Sgt Russell hit the right note when he said, 'Bewitched Bothered and Bewildered', because that's what a lot of the lads were. Many of the lads had never been away from home before, many were still homesick, some had lived in the country and had never seen a big city in their eighteen years, many were worried that their girlfriends would not wait for them and some of them had been deferred because they were serving apprenticeships. We were in for eighteen months at that time; many lads kept on saying, 'Roll on eighteen months' – little did we know that there was a shock to come later.

Chapter VIII

The Introduction to Carter Barracks at Bulford on Salisbury Plain, Wiltshire

WE DISEMBARKED AT SALISBURY RAILWAY STATION and were transported the few miles to Bulford; it was early evening when we arrived and as we passed through the main gate we only saw the sentry.

We were taken to the barrack spiders which were to be our new home for a while. We stood in ranks and as our names were called out and the battery we would be in, we fell in behind a bombardier (two striper). When all was completed we were allocated a bedspace in a barrack room.

I was very pleased to find that I was in 117 Battery, 'A' Troop, under Sgt Russell (infantry training), Sgt Williams (gunnery training), Sgt Brittain (assisting in most things) along with Bombardier Gillespie, Lance Bombardier O'Connel, Lance Bombardier Haylott and many of the lads who had become mates since arriving at Oswestry.

Facing our billet, about half a mile away, we could see Bulford Garrison (or as it was nicknamed 'Tin Town' because it was nearly all constructed of corrugated tin sheets). Also facing us on the hillside next to Tin Town was a giant kiwi, which had been cut out of the chalk, and we were told had been done by New Zealand troops who were stationed there during the War. The whole place seemed to be made of chalk, all through the stubbly grass you could see the chalk in the ground, and when you got a drink of water from the tap it was chalky white.

We were issued with bedding and then marched to the cookhouse for a meal. The women cooks were the first people we had seen – I don't know why but there was no one else about. We still didn't see anyone on the way back to the billets; the bombardiers then told us to spend a few hours getting ready for inspection by our Sergeant Major and officers on the morning parade.

At five-thirty in the morning there was such a commotion; someone was in the barrack room banging on a dustbin with a big stick and shouting,

'Come on you fucking wankers, hands off cocks, up with your socks and get out of them fucking wanking chariots.'

Dennis Tomlinson, who came from Castleford, shouted, 'Who the fuck is making all that noise? I can't sleep.'

'I am you horrible little nig nog,' shouted Sgt Brittain, 'Oh,' said Tomlinson, 'that's alright then, I didn't know we got woken up by the drums of the Artillery band.'

Washed, shaved and all looking smart we paraded outside at 0630 with our pint mugs, and were marched to the cookhouse (plates were supplied at the cookhouse) for porridge or cornflakes, sausage, tomatoes, egg & bacon, two slices of bread with a lump of butter, and the funny tasting tea we had been getting since coming into the Army.

Even though the weather was warm we still had to wear full battledress because of the women in the camp; other units would be in shirt-sleeve order at this time of year. At 0800 we were paraded on the barrack square where our officers were introduced to us: Captain Ball, Captain Davis, Lt Tony Claydon, Lt Chappel. We also met the RSM (Regimental Sergeant Major), RSM Baldock. We were inspected by our Battery Commander, Major Bayliss, who said it was a very good turnout.

Then came the Battery Sergeant Major, BSM Stamp, a small plumpish man with a very red complexion; it could be seen by his face that he was very bad tempered.

He proceeded to give us a lecture on the do's and don'ts of the camp, starting off by saying, 'You will at all times use the latrines, you will never have alfresco pisses and shits anywhere else in the camp. You will not at any time take my name in vain. You will not walk around this camp in shirt-sleeve order. You will not at any time fornicate or ride the regimental bike. If any of you are ever caught in bed with another man your feet will never touch the ground again. You will not flutter away you worldly goods by means of Brag, Pontoon or Poker. If I enter a barrack room you will immediately spring to attention. Don't ever tell me that anything is impossible, nothing is impossible and if I tell you to bring me a bucket of steam, you WILL bring me a bucket of steam. Now are there any questions about anything I have said?'

'Yes, sir,' said Gunner Weeks, 'what is alfresco pisses and shits?'

Sgt Major Stamp's face went redder, 'Are you fucking ignorant, lad?

Alfresco means out in the fresh air, so don't piss and shit all over Salisbury Plain.'

'What does anyone do if they are taken short?' asked Weeks.

'Shit yourself,' was the reply from BSM Stamp.

Ginger Payne who was standing behind me (he was from Pontefract, always having a joke) was overheard to say that if the Sgt Major thought nothing was impossible, he would like to see him stand on his head and shit down his back or even see him wipe his arse on a broken bottle; this set me of sniggering and it was all I could so to hide it.

'Any more questions?' asked the Sgt Major.

Weeks piped up again, 'Yes, sir, what is fornicating?'

I thought the Sgt Major was going to explode. 'Fornicating is having it off with women,' he said.

'Having what off?' said Weeks.

'Will someone please educate this lad to the ways of the world,' said the Sgt Major.

'Yes sir,' said Charlie Gladys, 'I'll tell him a few things this evening when we are cleaning our kit because he is in the next bed to me.'

Weeks then asked if it would be possible for him to borrow the regimental bicycle as he was a very keen cyclist. The Sgt Major thought that Weeks was taking the piss out of him, and told him in no uncertain terms that if he continued he would be charged with insubordination – Weeks even asked what that was.

The eighteen months we were serving were increased to two years and the Sgt Major announced it before he went off to his office. Gunner Marwood shouted that whoever the lousy bastard was who had increased our service should be shagged by a big woolly bull all the way around Salisbury Plain on the back on an army lorry.

The Sgt Major's reply was that he now had to stand all us brainless cunts for an extra six months.

Chapter IX

Kill the Enemy at all Times

TRAINING NOW STARTED IN EARNEST. We were all told what our occupations would be during our service, but first of all we had to become 'Gunners'.

I was to be trained as a wireless operator/field telephone and cable layer; some were to be drivers, generator operators, dispatch riders, but many would remain gunners. Sgt Russell was very good instructing us as infantry; it was drilled into us:

> The object of all weapon training is to teach a man the most efficient way to use his weapons and to kill the enemy at all times ... The main characteristic of the Bren gun is that it can be maintained and fired by one man in action.

Bayonet drill was very unusual, charging at straw dummies, screaming as you charged at them. Get your enemy down, said Sgt Russell, kick him in the bollocks, stamp on his head, stick your fingers in his eyes and up his nostrils, just make sure he is well and truly fucked. Tomlinson piped up and said, 'I thought we had to kill the enemy not fuck 'em.'

'Don't be a pillock,' said Sgt Russell, 'you know very well what I mean.'

The assault course was very rough, very hard chalky ground and if you jumped off any of the high obstacles it was easy to get sprained ankles.

Training with the different weapons, sten gun, Bren gun, rifle etc., became second nature. We got to the stage where we had competitions stripping and assembling them with a blindfold on.

Sgt Williams took us for our gunnery training. We were introduced to the 3.7 field gun and also to the 4.5 anti-aircraft gun. The 4.5 gun was a static gun with a big shield around it just like those on a ship; the 3.7 gun was used mostly by us as a field gun, but was also anti-aircraft and had been used throughout the War for that purpose.

We had it drilled into us until many of us dreamed about CRBBOs, LBMs, recuperators, firing mechanisms, breach block and many other parts of weapons, and tests required us to name all parts. Competitions were held amongst different batteries to see who got their gun into action first.

Top left then clockwise: *Gnr Barraclough; Gnr Jones; Gnr Edwards 442; Gnr Arkell.*

We would be travelling over Salisbury Plain in an AEC Matador (gun tractor) towing behind a 3.7 gun, the gun crew in the back of the matador. When the gunnery sergeant found a suitable place to put the gun, he would shout, 'Halt Action Rear,' the vehicle stopped, the crew jumped from the back and unhooked the gun, and the vehicle then drove away a short distance.

The crew would then lower the legs of the gun (which were on each corner), two men to each leg; they would then run round and round turning the raising screws (which were attached to the end of each leg) and lift the gun high enough to remove the road wheels. Having removed the wheels they would then run round and round turning the raising screws until the gun was flat on the ground; ground anchor pins were then sledge-hammered through holes at the base of the gun, the gun was levelled with a side clinometer (spirit level), the vehicle would come back and ammunition would be unloaded.

The procedure for getting the gun into action was repeated many times during a training session; running round the raising screws on the gun to lift it up and down made you very dizzy and sick, sometimes if it was near mealtime you couldn't eat. We became very proficient at getting a gun ready for action and mostly there was very little time between each team, seven or eight minutes in most cases.

At this time I had never even given it a thought, that as a signaller/radio operator I would be miles in front of the guns sending back 'Fire Orders'.

One young lad (who I will not name because of embarrassment to him) kept calling his rifle a gun, although Sgt Russell had told him about this on many occasions. 'A gun is a piece of artillery, a rifle is a long firearm or if you like to call it, a "Bundhook",' said Sgt Russell. 'Stop calling your rifle a gun.'

Sgt Russell pointed out the dangers of pointing a gun at anyone (loaded or not) and told us how dangerous a blank cartridge could be, saying that at close range a blank could penetrate a corrugated-iron sheet.

We had now got used to the camp. The NAAFI was in the middle, the barrack square was right in front of the NAAFI; the medical room was on the outskirts and was reputed to have been a morgue at some time; the gym was at the bottom of the camp behind the guard room.

Outside the camp gate if you turned left it went to Tidworth/Andover and to the right was a long straight stretch of road towards Salisbury/Lark-hill/Stonehenge.

The PTIs (Physical Training Instructors) had us running a mile along this straight stretch of road in PT kit. I feel sure that some of us eight-stone whippets broke the four-minute mile long before the record was noted; many times we ran the same stretch of road in full battle order.

The Women's Royal Army Corps worked as drivers/radar operators/cooks and cookhouse staff; all the drivers I ever saw were very good even on three-ton lorries.

Charlie Gladys came into the barrack room one day and told Gnr Weeks that he had just propositioned one of the women drivers.

'What do you mean?' said Weeks.

'Well I was walking past the cookhouse when one of the women drivers got out of a three-tonner. I asked her if she could drive; when she said yes I told her to put herself in reverse and back onto this,' said Charlie, sticking out his pelvis.

'What did she say?' asked Weeks,

'She said to me, can you fuck?' said Charlie. 'So I said, Yes. So she said, "Well fuck off, it's All Fools Day. Do you know," went on Charlie, 'I took that big blond woman corporal to the disused cricket pavilion by the Dumbelle Wood last night.'

'Don't tell me you shagged her,' said Weeks. 'She's so ugly her face would stop a clock.'

'Yes, I did and she thanked me afterwards. I like the ugly ones, no one has been with them,' said Charlie, winking at the rest of us. We knew he was having Weeks on just to impress him.

Charlie was one of the most inoffensive people I ever met, always jolly and never a bad word for anyone. He came from the Isle of Wight, was happily married and his stories about going with other women were all fictitious.

He was a very good and very keen motor cyclist, and was keen to get into the regimental trials team. He was told that he might get in after he had completed his training.

Chapter X

Charlie's Great Blunder

CHARLIE GLADYS HAD A VERY UNUSUAL TYPE OF GREETING. When he passed you he would say, 'Hello, Snake, how's your grandad's pot leg?' He also had a peculiar habit. If someone was bending down with their back to him he would rush up behind them, swing his arm in a circle, then give them a nip between the legs. He had done it many times and was known to many of the lads as 'Charlie the nut nipper'. We had told him that one day he would become a cropper, and that he might one day catch one of the woman officers, but he did not heed the warning.

The job of barrack room orderly was on a rota basis and each man took his turn. You were required to keep the barrack room tidy but the main reason was looking after everyone's kit (probably against theft). I was room orderly on one occasion and was cleaning my boots when in came a captain whose name I won't mention. He was over six feet tall, had a big ginger moustache, very red hair and a ruddy complexion.

I stood up to attention when he came in (you don't salute without your hat on). 'Carry on, Gunner Barraclough,' he said.

I carried on doing my boots and the Captain came up to my bedspace, remarking how my boots shone; he seemed very interested in my method of cleaning. He put his foot up on the bed rail and stood with his elbow on his knee, hand on his chin, his back to the door.

It would have to be me who was on room orderly that day, the biggest giggler in the Troop. Charlie had forgotten something and had returned to the room ... he saw a man with his back to him leaning over, so he came up the room at high speed swinging his arm in a circle ... I knew what was coming but was powerless to stop it. Charlie had nipped the Captain's nuts. I was absolutely bursting to laugh and was nearly choking trying to stifle it. The Captain nearly hit the roof as he spun round and screamed out, face as red as a beetroot, 'Gladys, what the fucking hell are you doing?'

Charlie was in shock and saluted with both hands, 'I'm very sorry, snake,' said Charlie (forgetting himself again). 'Sir, I mean, I thought you were one of the lads.'

'Oh, you make a fucking habit of indecently assaulting other men,' said the Captain.

'No sir, it's only a bit of fun,' said Charlie.

'So you think it's fun, do you, lucky for you I've got a sense of humour. Can you imagine the charge sheet?' said the Captain. ''2239???? Gunner Charlie Gladys to the prejudice of Good Order and Military Discipline in that you did on the said day grab a Royal Artillery officer by the goolies ...'

At this I was able to release my bottled up laughter and fell about laughing. The Captain thought that I was laughing at the way he worded the charge sheet but I was laughing at Charlie's blunder and the look of sheer shock on his face.

That night as we all sat cleaning our kit Charlie was telling all the lads how he had grabbed the Captain by the nuts. No one would believe him, so between my fits of laughter I convinced them that it was true. Word spread round the camp and a few days later some wag put a note on the Battery orders board in the corridor:

> Thou shalt not grab thy troop officer by the balls lest thy name be enrolled upon a 252 and a course of endurance shall be prescribed for thee.

It then said underneath: Try Battery Sergeant Major Stamp, a relative of Hitler.

We were all in bed, lights out had sounded but talking went on. One lad called out, 'Hey Charlie, you remember when the BSM said that anyone caught in bed with another man, his feet wouldn't touch the ground again?'

'Yes,' said Charlie.

'Why would any man get into bed with another man?' asked the lad.

'Because he would be a homosexual,' said Charlie.

'What's one of them?' said the lad.

'If you don't know, it's a man who shags men instead of women,' said Charlie.

'No one would do that,' said the lad.

'Yes,' said Charlie, 'they are called many different names.'

'Like what?'

'Oh, shirt lifters/queers/poofs/arse bandits/pile drivers, but it all comes down to one thing, they are dirty, perverted bastards,' said Charlie. 'Did you know that a lot of prostitutes were marching through London behind the Ban-the-Bomb campaigners; their placards said, Ban the Bum.'

'What's a prostitute?' asked the lad.

'Take no notice Charlie, he's taking the piss,' shouted someone else.

Then Weeks joined in, telling us that he had approached one of the officers who he had seen riding a bicycle, and asked if there was a cycling club. The officer had told him that there was, but it was for officers only. Weeks had then told the officer about the BSM's chat mentioning the 'Regimental bicycle'. He said that the BSM should have explained that the regimental bicycle was one of the women in the camp (naming her, but I won't), saying that most of the Regiment had been with her excluding our intake.

There were many ghost stories associated with Salisbury Plain. Men had seen a lady on a white horse crossing the plain, some had seen paratroops whose chutes hadn't opened (we were in the middle of a para training area). The medical room was supposed to be haunted and we had stories about people seeing Druids.

We had now come to the start of our occupations, which was done at first in between gunnery and infantry training including shooting on the ranges at Tidworth. Gunner Clegg who came from Pontefract (Tanshelf Drive) was a mate of mine, Cleggy we called him. He was told to get a haircut on parade one morning; it did not matter if you had only had you haircut the day before, the BSM told you anyway. You had to find time to go over to Tin Town to the barber. Cleggy couldn't afford the shilling that it cost, as we were always waiting for the next pay day. Cleggy knew that if he went on parade the next day without having his hair cut he would be on a charge, so he asked me to cut it for him.

I couldn't cut hair, but I tried with a razor blade and comb; the BSM nearly had a heart attack when he saw him and called him all the names he could think of.

'Who the fucking hell cut your hair, Clegg?' asked the Sgt Major.

'Gunner Barraclough, sir,' replied Clegg.

'Why did Barraclough cut your hair?' said the Sgt Major.

'Sir, you told me on parade yesterday morning that I would be on a charge if I didn't get my hair cut, and I couldn't afford the shilling until pay day,' said Clegg.

'With what did he cut you hair?' asked the Sgt Major.

'A comb and a razor blade,' said Clegg.

'Well, he has made a right fucking mess of it, you look like the last of the Mohicans,' said the Sgt Major.

Not very long after this we were doing PT in the gym. The instructors were having us do 'heaves to the beam' where you had to reach up, grab the beam above your head and heave yourself up until your chin was level with the beam. You had to do this as many times as you could. Some didn't have the strength in their arms to do it more than three or four times; Cleggy couldn't even get up once.

One of the instructors cupped his hands (as a jockey is helped onto a horse), and heaved Cleggy upwards, but Cleggy went over the top of the beam and landed on his head with a sickening thud.

There was panic among the instructors, Cleggy was taken away unconscious. When we asked about him later on we were told that he had been transferred to Gravesend in Kent. As eighteen-year-olds none of us were very wordly wise, but looking back now we never found out what had actually happened to Cleggy. I did write to his home address after my army service, but never got a reply.

Chapter XI

Guard Duties

W<small>E HAD BEEN LEARNING GUARD MOUNTING PROCEDURE</small> during our training and now had to do our first guard duty.

Alphabetical order, first name on the list, Gunner Arkell, then Barraclough, Bestwick and so on. It was the custom at that time that the smartest man on guard mounting was selected to be 'Attending man' (or as it was called, Stick Man); the man selected by the inspecting officer (orderly officer) didn't do the guard duty but fell out when the guard was dismissed, went back to his billet and got dressed in his denims (working clothes) after the guard had taken over the guard room from the old guard. The attending man would clean up the guard room, go to the cookhouse and collect the guard's supper, clean up again after supper then go back to his billet and bed.

At 0600 the following morning he would be at the cookhouse and collect the guard's breakfast; during the day he would be responsible for cleaning the guard room, polishing the 3.7 shell case (which was hanging upside down outside the guard room) used as a fire gong; he would then clean the guard room windows, go to the cookhouse for the dinner, clean up after dinner and was then free as the guard would dismount at 1800 hrs (6.00 p.m.).

We were marched to the barrack square by the guard commander, a sergeant, who could be from any battery. We got Sergeant Bayliss from 126 Battery.

The Orderly Officer was Mr Perret Young, a very tall and very smart officer. When he had inspected the guard he turned round and marched a few paces away, did a very smart about turn and faced us at attention.

He had made his selection of who would be attending man, and when he gave the order the attending man and the guard commander would step forward, right turn and march to the rear of the guard. 'Number two will be attending man,' he shouted. 'Guard Commander and attending man take post.'

The guard commander stepped smartly forward; I was a little slow because it hadn't sunk in properly that I was number two. Mr Perret Young shouted, 'Number two, if you want to be attending man move your fucking self.' I stepped forward and marched to my position behind the guard.

When I was dismissed I marched back to my billet; many of the lads had been having bets as to who would get the first attending man out of our troop; many had backed me.

After the 24-hour guard duty was over I vowed that I would never again go for attending man. Someone else could have the task of working like a horse.

When my next guard duty was posted on battery orders it was with Sgt Wingate who came from Leeds. When we arrived at the main gate the new guard stood facing the old guard. Sentries were changed, the old guard dismissed and Sgt Wingate marched into the guard room; he came back out with a clipboard.

Standing at the slope arms, rifle in his left hand, clipboard in his right he proceeded to read, 'Standing Orders for the guard of the 46th Heavy Ack-Ack Regiment, Royal Artillery at Carter Barracks, Bulford. You will be alert at all times. If you are approached by anyone you will shout "Halt Who Goes There". If the reply is "Friend" you will say "Advance friend and be recognised". If you don't get any answer, challenge again. If you still don't get an answer, take steps to wrap your fucking rifle around his neck. If anyone approaches the barrier in a vehicle, do not lift the barrier, make the occupant/s get out and come forward to be recognised. If he/they won't get out and tell you that they are the Colonel or officers of this Regiment, tell them that you don't care if they are Napoleon's fucking relatives. If you are approached during the night by an officer who asks you to let him examine your rifle tell him to fuck off, it may be the orderly officer, it may be an enemy ... don't fall for it. In the case of fire you will shout very loudly, "FIRE, FIRE" repeatedly at the same time pissing on it to try and extinguish it. Finally the NCO I/C marching relief [second in command] will change the prowler guard and the main gate guard at two-hour intervals. I will be sleeping because I am a selfish bugger ... To the Guard room, Dismiss.' If Sergeant Wingate is still living in Leeds he will verify this.

The main gate guard did two hours on, and four hours off; the prowler guard did the same but prowled around the eerie perimeter of the camp with a pickaxe handle. Many of us when on prowler guard would get into a haystack of which there were many all around the camp; some would go and sit in the MI room reading magazines until they were relieved, but after some ghostly happenings there no one would go near the place at night. I was not a believer until I saw for myself what happened one night. More about that later ...

Chapter XII

Sick Parade and the Crabs

THOMAS DENNIS HOLE (we called him 'Tot') came from Shildon, Co. Durham; he was twenty-six years old, eight years older than most of us and for some reason had been deferred. Five foot two and a very comical sort; on parade every morning there was a call for sick and defaulters to fall out.

One morning Tot decided to go and report sick. 'What's the matter with you,' asked Bombardier Gillespie.

'Well,' said Tot, 'I've niver had a twitch since I came in the Army and with all these women in the camp, I should have.'

'What are you on about?' said Bdr Gillespie.

'I canna get a fucking hard on,' said Tot.

'Ah!' said the Bombardier, 'you mean you can't get an erection,'

'Wayhi man,' Tot said in his Geordie accent.

'You don't need to go sick for that, it's the Bromide in you tea that causes that,' said the Bombardier, 'Haven't you ever noticed the taste of the tea.'

'Wayhi man,' said Tot, 'but who the fuck puts it in the tea.'

'The cooks,' said the bombardier.

'I'll be gan doon the cookhouse to have a word with those women,' said Tot.

One lad was constantly complaining of itching particularly around his privates. One of the Scots lads, Jock Pow, told us that at one time he had worked in a laundry; he said that it was possible that the lad had caught 'Crabs' and added that you could catch them from dirty laundry, or possibly from sleeping on mattresses on which some other persons suffering from crabs had slept. It was suggested that the mattresses in the guard room could be where he had caught them, because many soldiers slept on them during their off-duty hours.

Most of us had never heard of crabs (only seaside crabs). What are they? was asked. Jock Pow told us that they were tiny crab-like insects which got under the skin and caused very bad irritation and even got into the

34

hair. This young lad said that he had been sleeping on mattresses in the guard room and was going sick.

The MI Room was full when he reported sick, and the lad told us that the Medical Officer had called him in and left the door open. There were women in the waiting area as well as men; the MO had examined him and then shouted, 'Shave off, you've got the Sandy's.'

'Shave what off, and what's the Sandy's, sir?' the lad asked.

'Shave all the hair off you bollocks, chest and under your arms, lad, you've got the Sandy McNabs … Crabs.' he shouted for all to hear.

The young lad was very embarrassed as he walked through the waiting room to the treatment room. He told us that the medical orderly had helped him shave; he had then had to sit in a bathful of hot water and then had some white paste daubed on his private parts.

Those in the waiting room had heard all and some of the women were sniggering at him, he said. All his clothing was sent away to be cleaned; one of the bombardiers called him a dirty bastard and accused him of not having regular baths.

When you had a bath in our troop you had to go to an NCO and sign, the 'Bath Book'. This lad had bathed regularly, and it was established the mattresses in the guard room were to blame. The bombardier was made to apologise in public.

Some days later the camp wag (whoever he was) put another note on the wall in the toilets, just as he had put the note on the orders board about Charlie Gladys' blunder. It went:

When you enter this noble hall
Use the paper not the wall.
Do not stand upon the seat
The crabs in here can jump six feet.
Don't bother going in next door
The bastards there jump six feet four.

There were many diseases we had never heard of until coming into the Army; 'Pink Eye' was one of them and apparently you could get this by using someone else's towel. One of our lads had reported sick; the sly sod had been seeing the regimental bicycle unknown to any of us and nothing had been said that he was going to a hospital in Aldershot. He had packed all his kit and put it in the stores; apparently he was on the station at

Salisbury when one of our lads who had been home on compassionate leave saw him. This lad told us that he had shouted across to him from another platform and asked him if he was going on leave; he said he wished he had never asked because the reply he got shouted at him, with everybody in the station hearing it:

'Am I going on leave, boyo? No, I am not going on leave, I'm going to the pox doctor at Aldershot to have the umbrella needle; I've got a fucking nap hand boyo. Oh and by the way, boyo, keep away from poxy Annie, because that's where I have got it from. Talk about luck, I've got the luck of a pox doctor's clerk.'

We were asked if any of us would be prepared to got to Porton Down, an experimental establishment not far from where we were. Quite a few of the lads volunteered to take part in their scientific experiments, enticed by an extra one shilling a day. While there, they were infected with the common cold and then they were supposed to be cured with medicines.

Some days after they had returned, some of us who hadn't been caught bad colds; I was so badly infected that the MO had me sent into Tidworth Military Hospital where I spent a few days.

It was in the hospital there that I was told by one of the Queen Alexandra's Royal Army Nursing Corps about the 'Demon Drummer of Tidworth'. The story was that in the Middle Ages a beggar had walked around Tidworth, beating on a drum whilst begging; no one had given him anything so he had left the village and put a curse on the people.

Chapter XIII

Learning to be a Signaller

I WAS ASSIGNED TO BOMBARDIER NICHOLLS to be trained as a wireless operator/field telephone linesman, and all communications to do with the radar system. Bombardier Nicholls was a very pleasant chap and a very good instructor. He started lessons by teaching the phonetic alphabet, which I still remember: Able ... Baker ... Charlie ... Dog ... Easy ... Fox ... George ... How ... Item ... Jig ... King ... Love ... Mike ... Nan ... Oboe ... Peter ... Queen ... Roger ... Sugar ... Tare ... Uncle ... Victor ... William ... X-Ray ... Yoke ... Zebra. The radio sets were the 22 (twenty-two set) and required a twelve-volt battery which was in a wooden frame with carrying handles.

We had the phonetic alphabet drilled into us until we knew it by heart; the lads on the team would talk to each other in phonetic and all the others thought we were going barmy. Numbers were pronounced: Wun ... Two ... Thuree ... Fower ... Fiyive ... Sixer ... Sevven ... Eight ... Niner ... Zero. If you wanted to use capital letters in a message you would say, 'Blocks on' and to finish 'Blocks Off'.

So you would call to your mate over the air: hello Tare Uncle Baker Two Wun (your call sign), Hello Tare Uncle Baker Two Wun Message, Over. The reply would come back: Hello Tare Uncle Baker Two Wun, send your message, Over. You then gave the message: Hello Tare Uncle Baker Two Wun, meet me in the 'Blocks On' Nan Able Able Fox Item, 'Blocks Off' at Wun Sixer Hundred Hours. This meant 'Meet me in the NAAFI at 4 o'clock'. When you set up your radio net you had to send out a 'netting call' which went as: Tare Uncle Baker Tare Uncle Baker and you would repeat this until all your outstations had got you loud and clear, then you would say: Hello all stations Tare Uncle Baker, hear netting call, net now. You then held the microphone to your chest with the pressel switch pressed in, the other stations would turn their aerial dials to the highest reading they could get; after a few minutes you would tell them: Netting call ends. You would then call: Hello all stations Tare Uncle Baker, report my signals, Over. Each station would report what strength they were receiving you; strength nine was excellent; if any stations had not got a good signals strength or the signal was in any way distorted you would have to net them in again.

Field telephones and cable laying was very interesting as were the sound-powered phones and headsets used on the radar. Tannoy loud-speakers were set up near the guns to receive fire orders.

The radio set was fairly heavy and when going out on a scheme it was strapped to your back; you carried all the spare valves, aerials and micro-phones/earphones in satchels, and the battery between two men.

Field telephones Tele 'F', Tele 'H' and Tele 'J' were connected by don-eight wire (so called because it was constructed of seven strands of steel and one strand of copper wire); telephones were powered by batteries connected in series or parallel and when you cut the don-eight wire to pass it under railway lines, it was rejoined by what was called a semi-permanent joint.

Signals training went along very smoothly, and Bombardier Nicholls would send us out on our own to test us at setting up radio or telephone communications. Then came our first major test – we were taken to Bude in Cornwall for our first 'firing camp', Cleve Camp it was called, and this would be the first time that the new intake of 1950 would actually fire the 4.5 heavy anti-aircraft gun.

The guns were static, stood on concrete bases facing out to sea; I wouldn't be on the guns but would be looking after the communications side. There were many junction boxes on the static site to which we could connect our field telephones and tannoys, these being permanent. When you opened a junction box to connect any wiring, it was always crammed full of earwigs which you cold pick up by the handful.

We were at Bude for a month and were in tents. Now they always say that the first impression is a lasting one … Yes it rained at Bude nearly all the time we were there and my impression of the place was not very good.

In our spare time we had nothing to do, but we did get an invite to watch the Bofors guns doing a night shoot which was very good. Some evenings we went down onto the seafront for a walk, one evening being cut off by the tide and having to climb up a steep cliff face. Darkie Glover and his mate Gunner Miles (Birmingham and Wolverhampton) had got nearly to the top; I was just behind them when I lost my footing on a patch of loose stones and was slipping back down ... Darkie Glover reached down and grabbed me by the arm, hauling me to safety. Thanks again Darkie.

The toilets at Bude were of the bucket type, with a door at the bottom of the wall behind each toilet, which slid to one side when opened. Late at night the buckets were emptied (still don't know who by, but probably the permanent staff at the camp).

One night we had been to the NAAFI and on the way back to our tents one lad decided to go to the toilets (latrines). Apparently he had sat down and had not heard the men emptying the buckets, the bucket had been slid out from underneath him, emptied, and then slid back in, trapping his nuts between the seat and the bucket. His scream could be heard all over Bude. I now know why my father told me about Rule fifty-five: 'Never let them dangle,' he had said.

Everything went off without a hitch communications-wise, and all in all it had been an interesting month. As we left the camp our convoy was halted on the narrow roads leading into the town (which we had not seen during our stay). There was a man on a big white horse dressed as an army Major. 'Get all you vehicles up onto the grass verge,' he said. 'There is another convoy coming the other way into the camp.' After sitting there with the lorries halfway up the verge for about an hour, a don-R (dispatch rider) was sent to see where this other convoy had got to. Not having found any signs of another convoy he had contacted the local police. 'Was it a chap on a white horse who told you?' asked the police. 'Yes,' said the don-R. 'You have met the village idiot,' said the police. Our officers were very annoyed and said he should be locked up for impersonating an officer, but what can you do with a nutter?

Chapter XIV

The Firing Ranges at Tidworth and More Infantry Training

BACK AT BULFORD WE CONTINUED WITH INFANTRY TRAINING. Sgt Russell had taught us how dangerous the 9mm Sten machine carbine (Sten gun) was. He demonstrated this by holding a Sten gun away from his body at arms length and with a full magazine banged the butt of the hard ground – the whole magazine blasted off into the air without the trigger being touched. He said that men had fallen over fences while carrying a Sten gun and had been wounded or killed by letting it strike the ground ... he said that the gun was unreliable and to be very careful when using it ... it also had a reputation for jamming. 'If your gun jams while you are firing it on the ranges, do not, and I repeat, do not swing round and point the gun towards the rest of the personnel and say "Sergeant, my gun has jammed", it might just go off and kill some of us.'

The young man who kept on calling his rifle a gun still continued to do so. We were firing on the ranges at Tidworth and this lad said he couldn't get the clip of bullets into his gun. Sgt Russell called him over. 'Do you know,' he said, 'they had a cure in the American Marines for people who called their rifle a gun.'

'What was that?' asked the lad.

'Take out your prick,' said the Sergeant. 'Now take your prick in your left hand and take your rifle in you right hand. Now run around the safety area and chant "In my right hand is my rifle, in left hand my gun, one is for fighting and one is for fun".'

The lad got into the spirit of the joke and was running around chanting ... everyone was in hysterics. The lad was near the entrance to the ranges very near to the main road when an Austin light utility (Tilly) came past full of WRACs with an officer sat next to the driver. It stopped and the officer got out. On approaching the lad, she asked him what he was doing. 'In my right had is my rifle, in my left had is my gun, one is for fighting and one is for fun,' he chanted. She was going to have him charged with indecent exposure until the Sergeant told her what was going on. She thought it was hilarious and so did all the other women.

On the way back to Bulford and having fired the rifle/Bren and Sten guns, we were told about 'Aircraft Action': 'Aircraft don't like small arms fire,' said Sgt Russell. 'When I blow my whistle, as we cross the Plain, the Bren-gunners will stand where they are and pretend to fire at an imaginary aircraft ... the number two on the Bren will pretend to change the magazines ... all the riflemen will double away one hundred yards, drop onto one knee and pretend to fire at the imaginary aircraft.' Suddenly he blew the whistle and shouted, 'Aircraft Action'. Everyone did as they should except one lad. We carried on again after Sgt Russell had told the lad that he had to double away one hundred yards. The order was given again ... this lad did the same thing again and just knelt down by the Bren-gunners ... so it went on. Sgt Russell asked the lad what the idea was. 'Can't be bothered to play at fucking silly games firing at an imaginary aeroplane,' said the lad. 'Oh!' said Sgt Russell, and marched us back to camp. Being the mild-mannered man that he was, Sgt Russell didn't put him on a charge, but it was plain to see that it wasn't finished there.

We had our evening meal at about 5.30 p.m., got back to the billets and started to clean our kit ready for the next morning. One of the bombardiers came in cursing and swearing. 'Everyone get dressed in FSMO (Field Service Marching Order). You will put in your big pack two folded blankets; in your small pack you will put your PT kit, towel, soap, razor. In your ammunition pouches you will put sand from the maintenance yard at the rear of the camp. Wear your overcoat, steel helmet and carry your rifle. You will parade outside in twenty minutes, courtesy of the man who thought it was playing silly games firing at an imaginary aircraft.'

All outside, Sgt Russell called us to attention. 'Right, my lucky lads,' he said, 'Gunner H ... needs to be taught that in the Army, and especially in action, one man can fuck it up for all his comrades by disobeying a direct order. I don't put men on a charge because if they get 156 days in Shepton Mallet or Colchester it will add the time to their military service. So I give the whole troop a lesson ... in turn the troop will give the offender a lesson.'

We were marched to the barrack square ... it started to rain very heavily ... round and round the square we marched, overcoats getting heavier, our nicely blancoed webbing washed out. Many officers had come to look out of the windows of their quarters. They must have thought it was some kind of an endurance test. Eventually we were marched back to the billets – no one would be going to the NAAFI that night, including the NCOs.

We were up nearly all night drying our kit and getting it ready for the morning's inspection ... What would be the revenge on Gunner H ... ?

We were sat cleaning our kit a few nights later when the lad who had been calling his rifle a gun called across the room, 'Hey Charlie, you know that woman officer who saw me on the ranges with my prick out.'

'What about her?' asked Charlie.

'Well she keeps smiling at me when I pass her,' said the lad.

'Good for you, boy, get in there; she's seen your tackle and now fancies you,' said Charlie.

There was always good fun in the barrack rooms at night. Ginger Payne and Denis Tomlinson were good mates but were in different rooms. One evening Tomlinson went into the room where Ginger was, taking his rifle with him; they must have been sat cleaning their kit and rifles, chatting, keeping each other company.

Next morning we were called out for rifle drill, but Tomlinson couldn't find his rifle (probably forgot he had taken it with him the night before).

'Where's your rifle?' asked the Bombardier.

'I heven't getten noan,' said Tomlinson in his broad Yorkshire accent.

'What did you say?' asked the Bombardier.

'I heven't getten noan,' said Tomlinson.

'Can anyone interpret this Yorkshireman for me?' Asked the Bombardier.

Ginger Payne piped up and said, 'He's Baht' (as in Ilkely Moor baht hat): without, in other words. The Bombardier was no wiser ...

Chapter XV

Ghosties, Ghoulies, Wee Willie Winkies and Things That Move in the Night

I WAS DOING A PROWLER GUARD, and was being marched up the camp to relieve the previous guard who had just done his stint from midnight to two o'clock. He wasn't where he should have been, but the lights were on in the old MI room which was reputed to have been a morgue. Many of the men had gone and sat in there during their stint on prowler, instead of prowling the camp perimeter; it helped to pass the time reading the magazines in the waiting room.

The Bombardier I/C marching relief and I were about to enter the building when this lad came past us at speed; the Bombardier shouted for him to stop, but he ignored him and kept running. As we entered the MI room the lights went off. 'Someone's in there,' said the Bombardier. 'Get your pickaxe handle ready.' I found the light switches near the door and switched on the lights. We searched every inch of that MI room but found nothing, not a sign of anyone ... suddenly the lights went off again. We knew that no one was near the switches ... so we left there fast. There was a clatter of hobnailed boots – Sgt Bayliss and the rest of the guard were running up the camp with rifles and pickaxe handles at the ready.

Sgt Bayliss saw the Bombardier and myself and shouted in his deep, gravelly voice, 'What the fuck is going on? We've just had a man bursting into the guard room jibbering and pointing up the camp. We can't get any sense out of him.'

'He's probably seen a ghost,' said the Bombardier.

'Don't talk like a cunt, there is no such thing as a fucking ghost,' said Sgt Bayliss.

'Perhaps there is no fucking ghosts,' said the Bombardier, 'but there are certainly ordinary ghosts.'

Sgt Bayliss heard our account of what had occurred and went into the MI room, put the lights on, had a look around and the lights went off.

He put the lights on again and then put them off again to test the switches (they were the very old brass type) and very strong. It would have been impossible for all six switches to be faulty at once and go up on their own. He stood watching the switches after he had put them on again … there was one click … and off they went again … So did Sgt Bayliss. So did we all. Never to go there again at night. It was agreed that we all tell the other lad that the switches were faulty … he would never be convinced.

As all the guard were now fully awake, the ones who were off duty decided that the lad who had caused us the punishment parade would now pay. The double doors into the barrack room were opened and he was carried out (sleeping soundly) still in his bed and was placed in the middle of the WRAC wash room. What a shock the women would get when they went for a wash. What a shock he would get when he woke up. We found out later that when the women had found him in their washroom they had brought out their CSM, Company Sergeant Major Mallard, who had ordered him out. He said he couldn't because he slept in the nude. No one ever found out who had moved him and even Sgt Bayliss kept quiet about it.

Unknown to the rest of us the lad had not yet had all his punishment. We all had a shelf over the top of our beds, on which were your mess tins and best boots. Some of the NCOs who had suffered for his stupidity had been pissing in his best boots. There was a very bad smell in the barrack room, and no one could pinpoint it except for the fact that it was strongest near this lad's bed. It was not often that we wore our best boots or used our mess tins; they were there on the shelf all shiny.

One of the NCOs came in and shouted up the room that we would need our best boots all nice and shiny for the morning parade. He then walked out trying to hide his mirth while someone remarked about it, wondering why he was amused.

When we got our best boots down from the shelf this lad got drenched in a foul-smelling liquid – what a stench! The Sergeant Major called in and remarked that the room stank like a 'Persian Brothel' (how would he know?). 'Whatever it is,' he shouted, 'clean it up.'

The NCO came back in and shouted, 'Cancel the order about the best boots.'

Next morning, on the first parade, the lad told the Battery Commander that he had a very serious complaint to make. 'What is it?' asked the officer.

'Someone has been pissing in my boots and my uniform and shirt needs cleaning.'

'What do you expect me to do about it? Get on with it and get your uniform cleaned. Oh, and by the way,' said the officer, 'Someone once pissed in my boots at Sandhurst.'

'Did you find out who had done it?' said the lad.

'No,' said the officer, 'I just went round and pissed in everyone else's boots in the hope that I would get the culprit eventually.'

We had got our first 48-hour pass, and all those who could get home went for the weekend (obviously a 48-hour pass wasn't much good for the Scots lads). It wasn't much good to Yorkshire lads but it was there and we took it. Gunner Huttley had been home and had missed his train to Salisbury, which meant that he would miss the duty driver and a lift back to camp, so he caught another train and got out at Andover. He then walked from Andover to Bulford. He told of how he had encountered a man dressed in medieval clothes and beating on a drum. The man had said to him just one word, 'Alms'. Gnr Huttley said the hair at the back of his neck stood on end, because as he put his hand in his pocket to find a couple of pennies for the man he just disappeared into thin air. He said from that point he had made record time from Tidworth to Bulford. Gnr Huttley was a big lad and when some of the others made fun of him he threatened to thump them.

I then told them what the nurse at Tidworth Military Hospital had told me. She lived in the nurses' quarters in Tidworth. Could it be possible that there is any folklore in Tidworth about the 'Demon Drummer'? It was eerie on Salisbury Plain, and it didn't help having a pack of hounds howling every night. These hounds were across near the garrison Tin Town. Who they belonged to we never found out. Were they hunting hounds belonging to some local hunt? Or were they something to do with the officers? Did they have a private hunt? Either way, if any of us had got our hands on a grenade, it would have gone in.

Chapter XVI

The Battle of Weybourne

Dear John. Sorry I am going out with your Mate

WE HAD COME INTO THE ARMY FOR EIGHTEEN MONTHS and it had been increased to two years. Girlfriends couldn't wait and many were now sending 'Dear John' letters which the lads pinned up on the orders boards. I never got a letter, although I was engaged to a girl who was going with another chap behind my back; I found out from another source.

One lad had been home on a forty-eight hour pass and was delighted to tell us that his girlfriend was six months pregnant. Charlie Gladys told the lad that it couldn't be his because had just been home for the first time in seven months. 'Who is it then?' asked the lad.

'It's a vengeance baby,' said Charlie.

'What's a vengeance baby?' asked the lad.

'Someone must have had it in for you,' said Charlie.

Some girls were going out with lads who had been mates, those who had not passed the medical or were unfit. Some of the lads said good riddance, some said they would ring their mates' necks.

We travelled to Weybourne, Norfolk by train for our second firing camp and had a lot of fun travelling there because we were all mixed, men and women. Bombardier Nicholls told me in confidence that I was to be promoted to lance bombardier. He was only six months from his release date, and said that I would be taking over from him as signals instructor if all went well.

We marched from the station at a little place called 'Holt' right to the camp. When we arrived we found that American servicemen were stationed there. Once again we were in tents, bell tents with six men to a tent plus all their kit. The 4.5 guns were on the coast, right next to them were some bigger calibre guns; these had a cellar underneath them and the ammunition for them was sent up from the cellar by lift.

The target at which we fired was a 'sleeve' which was towed through the air behind an aircraft on a long steel winch cable (pity the poor buggers in

Outside the cookhouse tent at Wexbourne, Norfolk.
Left to right: *Yorkie [?]; Charlie Bonner; Wright [?]; Barraclough [?].*

the plane). The first shoot proved to be a classic – our WRAC were manning the radar equipment ... the girls on the tracker/predictor had got the target in their telescopes ... the predictor passed its information to the tactical control, which in turn passed information to the fire control ... fire control sent its information to the guns ... when the gunners saw the dials on the gun moving they had to black out and match up their dials with radar. When they had blacked out and matched up it was just a matter of following the dials. All was ready to fire when the order was given. All communications were in good working order, having cleaned hundreds of earwigs from the junction boxes. The weather station at Bawtry had given us a 'meteor', which when fed into the radar determined the state of the weather – course or fine, wind speed and direction – and worked out where the shell would meet the sleeve. 'Fire' came the order. All three batteries fired together. At that time there were no earmuffs to deaden the sound. Some of us are now in our seventies and very deaf, which I say was caused by gunfire.

47

Having nothing to do and with all communications working well, Bombardier Nicholls and I volunteered to be safety men. This entailed sitting on the hillside behind the guns with a large board which was laid on the ground facing out to sea. On the board there was an arc pencilled onto a big sheet of paper – if any ship came into the arc we had to call for a ceasefire until they had passed. We watched the shellbursts in the sky, bursting all around the sleeve. Suddenly the sleeve seemed to jerk, snapped from the cable and came floating very slowly down. Cease fire came as the command target was destroyed. Normally the sleeve would have dropped into the sea but this sleeve came floating gracefully down and landed right on the barrel end of the 117 Battery gun – 124 and 126 Batteries women said that they hit the sleeve and were claiming it as a trophy. Three batteries couldn't all have it, so 117 Battery said that they would claim it because of where it landed. None of the women were having that so they charged in force into 117 Battery's gun position. All hell broke loose … I never saw a fight like that in my life. I will never see another like it. Women's Royal Army Corps? More like women from hell … scratching, biting, pulling each other's hair out in lumps, kicking and punching … many having a tug of war with the sleeve … many with their legs all over the place and not bothered about showing their knickers. 'Get in there and stop them,' Company Sergeant Major Mallard shouted to Sgt Major Stamp.

'Fuck off,' shouted Sgt Major Stamp, 'I would rather get into a cage full of wild fucking lions.'

'Fucking chicken,' shouted CSM Mallard, 'Someone will have to stop them.' The men of all three batteries crowded onto the hillside to watch this spectacle, cheering and egging them on, and also making very crude remarks, which I will leave to your imagination.

All the fighting proved to be of no avail, because the sleeve was sent back to wherever they were supplied from, to be repaired and used again.

The regimental bicycle had been for a night out in Sherringham, and returned to camp late in the night. We were still doing guard duties even at these camps, our guard room being a small marquee. She had come into the guard room claiming to have been raped. 'Raped? Raped?' shouted the guard commander. 'You have been raped? I don't believe it … more likely that you have raped some poor sod' (it was because of her reputation). She demanded that he call the women's orderly officer, so he telephoned her

Beans and Chips supper in the Naafi at Weybourne, Norfolk. Author is sat on the right.

and explained the situation. The women's orderly officer duly arrived bringing with her the MO (Medical Officer) who examined the woman in another tent.

Next morning, every military unit in the Norfolk area was visited by the civilian police and Pte ??????? was taken with them to identify the rapists. When our battery was paraded for the benefit of the police, the Sergeant Major shouted, 'Take one step forward all those who have been with Pte. ???????.' It was amazing how many men stepped forward, particularly amongst those who would soon be leaving the Army.

It mattered not to the police if she had been with the whole regiment, a crime had been committed. She did pick out two men from another unit and it was some months later, after we were back at Bulford, that we heard the men had got three years each.

There were a few incidents to mention while we were at Weybourne, like the time we were firing and a ship came into the arc of fire; we called for a ceasefire and one officer called, 'Put a fucking shot across his bows, that will make him move.' The fight in the little village pub (The Ship)

This could be the last pillbox at Weybourne, Norfolk.

between Americans and British soldiers. This was caused by one of the American soldiers calling Sgt Williams a 'Fucking Limey'. For some unknown reason he had taken a dislike to Sgt Williams and had said very loudly that if it wasn't for the stripes on that fucking Limey's arm he would do him. That was his mistake, Sgt Williams took off his battledress blouse and told the Yank that he no longer had the stripes on his arm. What a free-for-all that was, with Sgt Williams nearly throwing the Yank through the window as mates from both parties joined in. All in all the American soldiers in the camp were very good lads, but of course you always get one or two from all walks of life causing trouble. Some of the Americans were astounded when they heard how much pay we got ... some even brought us cartons of cigarettes over to our tents.

One evening I was crossing the camp when I encountered an old mate from home; he was in another regiment – officer's batman, he said ... Eric Smalley he was called – I arranged to meet him one Saturday evening to go for a drink in Sherringham. He turned up with a white raincoat on, and when he took it off in the pub he was dressed in his captain's uniform. I told him that it was a serious offence to impersonate an officer, but he said he did it regularly when his captain went off for the weekend. He said it was a good way of 'Pulling the posh birds'.

Chapter XVII

The Underground Shelter, Dumbelle Wood and the Cricket Pavilion

Back at bulford we kept on having days of infantry training just behind our billets (about 200 yards). There was an underground air-raid shelter which had been there since early on in the War. To get into it you had to walk down a long steep slope, the slope levelled out at the bottom and ran horizontal for about one hundred yards. Every so far along the tunnel there were doorways leading into small cells. In each cell there were rusty bunk beds which folded against the walls. It was pitch dark inside the tunnel and this is where we learned to do the 'Ghost Walk'.

You were taught to walk flailing your outstretched arms and legs to feel for obstacles in the dark. We were following each other at intervals into the tunnel about three yards apart. About halfway through the tunnel someone would give you an almighty clout on the top of your steel helmet nearly knocking your head into your shoulders. Then you would hear someone giggling as though it was a great big joke. Gunner Douglas Gordon Goody, (how famous he was a few years later) got a heavy blow on his shoulder. This was because he was so tall and whoever it was dishing it out was smaller. It was thought that a cosh was being used (it turned out to be a sock full of sand). Now I don't know who, but someone who had caught it in the tunnel, crept back in. Creeping along the tunnel and going from doorway to doorway he had come to where the blows were being struck. Eyes now accustomed to the darkness he had

L/Bdr Douglas Gordon Goody 1950s. Douglas became famous some years later.

waited for the next thud, and had then struck. 'How are the mighty fallen in the midst of the battle?'

Outside we were all lined up and the biter who had been bitten wanted the 'Son of a bitch' who had got him. Douglas Goody said to him, 'Yes I agree with you, Sergeant, because if I get the lousy bastard who hit me, I'll kick his bollocks up into his throat …'

The Dumbelle Wood was at the other side of the track from the shelter; the old, disused, dilapidated cricket pavilion stood with its back to the wood … there was no glass in the windows of the pavilion, and we were required to run past and lob a dummy grenade through the front window. The grenades were dropping onto the floor of the pavilion, and the officer was stood looking into a rear window to see how we fared. One lad ran past and lobbed his grenade … he completely missed the window … his grenade ran up the sloping roof … tottered on the apex … which way was it going to go … would it roll back down … no, it rolled over and went down the other side. It was a good thing the officer's cap was well padded because it hit him right on top of his head.

Did this annoy him? I don't know, but he had us charging through the thickest part of Dumbelle Wood which was one tangled mess of brambles and nettles. It was a good thing we were in denims, because many of us had torn clothing and scratches.

About this time I was summoned to a cadre course along with some other lads. The RSM wanted to be satisfied that we could make ourselves heard, could command a troop of men marching and drilling, and could call them to halt (as the left foot passed the right). He had us bawling and shouting very near to a generator which was on at full blast; he took us individually with rifle drill; he tested us on sentry drill. When he was satisfied that we could do all these things, he posted the promotions on the battery order, which meant that we would now be responsible for the guard duties, as many of the guard commanders liked to have a sleep, and taught the second in command how to make out guard reports.

We had many interesting signals schemes with Bombardier Nicholls. Cable laying was particularly interesting; digging it in across farm gates; weighting it down with bricks so that it went down the sides of river banks and across the bottom, so as not to foul boat propellers; cutting it and passing under railway lines then rejoining it. The Army was becoming very interesting, although many said it was a waste of time.

Some were like Charlie Gladys: happy go lucky. Charlie couldn't care less. Rumours were going round that we were to move, no one knew where to. We got our seven days leave in due course; when all leave was over and everybody had been home we suddenly got the order to move: we were going to Surrey.

A couple of days before we moved, we were invited to go and watch a demonstration of Royal Air Force Typhoons; some unit had put tanks/old buses and cars in a field near to the Royal Artillery school of gunnery at Larkhill. Some big wig had landed in the field next to where we were in his Auster light aircraft. The School of Artillery fired coloured smoke shells to each corner of the target area and rocket-firing Typhoons – what a sight – came diving down firing their rockets as they came. The skill of those pilots was astounding.

Two days later we were saying Goodbye to Bulford.

Chapter XVIII

Hello Hobbs Barracks

IT WAS MID-AFTERNOON WHEN WE ARRIVED at our camp. The signboard had already been erected at the main gate: 46th HAA (M) Royal Artillery. There was a lovely smell of freshly baked bread in the air – a Royal Army Service Corps bakery just over the road from the main gate. Turning into the gate it was a one-way system round the camp ... speed limit 5 miles per hour. Going to the left up the camp were woods on the left, RSM's office and stores on the right. Travelling to the top of the camp the Colonel's house and gardens on the right at the road junction ... barrack square and officers quarters ... turn along the road at the very top of the camp ... straight on ... at the side another barrack square ... sergeants' quarters ... MT and gun sheds ... NAAFI ... coal yard ... coming down the right side ... cookhouse ... barber's shop ... butcher's shop (disused brick-built air-raid shelter) ... come to another junction, turn left to go back to the main gate ... stores ... joiner's shop ... Denis Tomlinson's favourite place, ration stores and armoury ... behind these the other half of the wood ... the centre of the camp was barrack rooms ... boiler houses. This was Hobbs Barracks, Lingfield, Surrey. Little did we know much fun was going to be had ...

If you went through a small part of the wood by the NAAFI, it brought you onto the football pitch which was in the middle of a horse racing gallops track (not to be confused with Lingfield Racecourse).

I was now allocated a room on my own, which was part of the barrack room but was partitioned off. I was now in charge and had to sign an inventory taking all the lockers, beds, wardrobes, tables etc. onto my charge ... if anything got nicked I would pay.

A couple of weeks after arriving at Hobbs Barracks, Gunner Carrol went AWOL. So did Gunner Neary, an Irish lad who came from Huddersfield. There was another deserter from one of the other batteries called Wood, I had never met him because he had deserted before I came into the Army.

We had not been having church parades at Bulford but we started to have them here. On the first Sunday we paraded outside the billets. 'Fall out the Roman Catholics ... fall out the C of E ... fall out the agnostics and nonconformists,' shouted the BSM. There were plenty of non-believers who didn't fancy going to church. All the non-believers were put on fatigues: peeling spuds in the cookhouse ... cleaning toilets ... cutting grass ... cleaning windows and many other jobs. Lo and behold, the following Sunday everybody had a religion.

One morning the Sergeant Major came to the door of the barrack room and bawled at the top of his voice, 'Get outside for muster parade all you bastards, last man out will be on a charge.' No one wanted to be on a charge but knew that BSM Stamp didn't joke (the bad-tempered little sod). Some lads even jumped out of windows so as not to be last. They needn't have bothered – one lad remained where he was. When it was found he was missing I was asked where he was (one of my lot). I looked in the barrack room and there he was. 'Come on,' I said, 'didn't you hear the BSM?'

'Yes,' he said, 'but he shouted "outside all you bastards" and I'm not a bastard.'

I said, 'Well, you know what the Sergeant Major is like ... figure of speech and not meant in the way you took it.' The lad came outside and stood there under a barrage of verbal abuse from the BSM. 'You, lad, are on a fucking charge,' shouted the BSM, 'why didn't you come out like the rest of them men.'

'Because, sir, you shouted "outside all you bastards".'

'So what,' said the BSM.

'I am not a bastard,' said the lad, 'my parents were married, but when everyone ran out I never knew there were so many bastards in our troop.'

'Report to the Battery Office in the morning in best battledress ... you're on a charge,' said the BSM.

'Right, sir,' said the lad, 'but I will be writing to the MP for the forces, a Mr Bellinger, I believe. I will demand an apology for the insult to my parents.'

'Oh,' said the BSM, 'it seems we have a fucking barrack room lawyer.'

The lad spoke to the troop officer during the day and someone must have taken his threat very seriously, the charge was scrubbed.

There was a war going on in Korea, and I applied for a posting to go there. My Battery Commander sent for me. 'Are you barking mad?' he asked.

'No sir,' I said.

'You must be,' he said, 'there is a war going on in Korea.' He took my posting application and tore it up, throwing it in the waste bin. 'That's what I think of your application,' he said.

'When Bombardier Nicholls leaves us, you will take over as I/C Signals, training other young men as signallers. You will of course be promoted to full bombardier. Be a good fellow,' he said, 'don't apply for a posting again. Bombardier Nicholls has recommended you as his successor.'

That was that. On the next battery orders was the name Thomas Denis Hole, posted to Korea ... the barrack room lawyer, as the BSM had called him, was posted to Manobier. Troublemaker, the BSM said ... we knew he wasn't.

'You lucky sod,' shouted one of the lads, 'Manobier, that's in Africa, isn't it?'

'Don't be a cunt,' shouted Taffy Edwards 442, 'Manobier is in Wales.'

Some of us were selected to attend a service at St Paul's Cathedral, to commemorate a Roll of Honour to the American dead, killed in the war ... new uniforms were issued to us, and drill was practised to get us used to marching with military bands. It was a very memorable day in my military service ... I was stood at the end of one pew, near to the aisle and was able to see all the dignitaries as they passed. As the queue of dignitaries slowed down behind each other I can say that I was stood for a moment shoulder to shoulder with the very highly esteemed, late, Sir Winston Spencer Churchill. There was also a film star I used to see in films when I was younger, Douglas Fairbanks junior.

Some time after that the Regiment was asked to assist in making the opening scenes to a film called *Sound Barrier*. It was to star Ann Todd and David Niven, and was made by London Films. I don't know what happened but David Niven didn't appear in the film, it was Ralph Richardson. We had a lot of good fun in helping with the scenes and also travelling to and from the location, which was Seaford, on top of what are called 'The Seven Sisters' (white cliffs). It wasn't very far to travel from Lingfield to Seaford. This was the first time for many a month that we servicemen had seen cream buns and cakes, which were supplied by the film company's canteen van.

The film crew would sit in awe as some of the lads told stories of their upbringing. I don't think that many of them realised what it was like to be poor; even some of our young officers and ones from universities hadn't a clue about the working classes. One lad told of how he had to sleep six in a bed (four brothers and two sisters) and three of them were 'bedwetters', he went on to tell us that the mattress was the 'flock-filled type' explaining that flocks (for those who didn't know) were small balls of woolly material … there was a big hole in the middle of the bed, where the piss had rotted the mattress, he said, and if you didn't hang on you were liable to fall through it. He then added (jokingly) that he always tried to sleep at the shallow end because he was a non-swimmer. Toilet paper, he said was something they never heard of … newspapers were cut up into squares and threaded on a piece of string, then hung behind the toilet door … if the outside toilet was frozen up during the winter they had a 'piss bucket', because inside toilets were unheard of in poor areas. I think a lot of the 'silver spoon' people (snobs) as we called them, knew nothing about the working class and looked down on them.

We had an extra guard duty at a place away from our camp, called Shirley Park, near Croydon. Every so often, when it was our turn to guard it, we went there by lorry and stayed for twenty-four hours, taking our rations with us. It was a wartime gunsite with a lot of valuable equipment on the site. I usually did the cooking because none of the others were much good at it. One night we were sat listening to Radio Luxembourg, a very popular station with the soldiers of the 1950s. It was on 208 metres on the medium wave and played all the modern songs. The sentry on the gate shouted, 'Turn out the Guard.' We all thought it was the orderly officer coming to make a snap inspection, as they did on many occasions and to see if you were alert. I awakened the guard commander who wasn't very pleased and arose shouting, 'What the fucking hell is going on?' On getting outside we found the sentry arguing with a man who spoke with a plum in his mouth (posh). The man was complaining that our Radio Luxembourg was far too loud. He didn't ask in a polite manner for us to be a bit quieter, he threatened that he would call the police and gave us a lot of verbal abuse, saying that soldiers thought that they could do as they pleased, but said he would not tolerate it. Our ginger-headed guard commander (who I won't name) had a very red complexion to start with. At first he tried to appease the complainant, and apologised for any disturbance, but the man just carried on with his tirade of abuse. Ginger got redder and redder … we had seen him in a temper before. Then in a very sarcastic manner he asked the man, 'Did you live around here in wartime, sir?'

'Yes I did,' said the man.

'Were you not away from home serving your country, sir?' said Ginger.

'No,' said the man.

'Did you come to this gunsite when the ack-ack guns were constantly blasting at enemy aircraft night after night, and did you then complain about the noise, sir?'

'No,' said the man.

'Well,' said Ginger, 'if you haven't fucked off in two minutes, I will stick my boot up your arse to the third fucking lacehole, and you can call who the fuck you like.' Nothing further was ever heard.

Chapter XIX

More of the Carryings On at Hobbs

THE NAAFI STAFF WERE ALL MEN who dressed in cooks whites (like the RASC bakers). We were stood paraded outside our billets while the troop officer was addressing us when a young lad dressed in cook's whites walked by, hands in his pockets and whistling – he didn't give us a second glance. The troop officer finished what he was telling us then added, 'And you won't walk around the camp with your hands in your pockets whistling, like the fucking RASC do.' The young lad didn't take any notice and carried on walking.

'Hey you, laaaad, did you hear what I said?' shouted the officer, but the lad still sauntered on. The officer then sent one of the bombardiers to bring the lad to him, he was brought back and the officer proceeded to give him a right bollocking. 'Who do you think you fucking well are? Do you always walk past an officer without saluting; you fucking RASC types think you own this camp; give me your name and number, I'm going to have you on a charge.'

'Don't understand you, what are you going on about?' asked the lad. 'I don't have a number. I'm NAAFI staff!' What a picture the officer's face was ...

The manager at the NAAFI was a little fat man who always seemed to be drunk during the evening. One of our lads was courting a WRAC corporal and they had gone behind the coalyard which backed on to the NAAFI. There was a flight of seven steps to the back door of the NAAFI where this lad and the girlfriend were having a cuddle (as they told it). They were down to the side of the steps when the NAAFI manager came out and stood at the top of the steps. The couple kept very quiet – how could they have known that it was a habit of the NAAFI staff to come out of that door and piss over the side of the steps? The NAAFI manager lit a cigarette, stood smoking for a minute and then pissed all over them; of course he didn't know they were there in the darkness. When the lad came into the barrack room he really did smell and couldn't find a name bad enough to call the NAAFI manager. Little fat bastard, he said ... get my own back, he said. We now knew what the horrible smell was as we passed behind the NAAFI to get to the football field – it must have been going on for a long time.

Some time later our troop officer asked if anyone had been behind the NAAFI in the dark – no one had. But it was known to us that the lad who had got drenched was having all his mates pissing in a fire bucket which he had hidden behind the hut ... Our troop officer said that someone had thrown a bucket of foul-smelling liquid over the NAAFI manager ... all the lads who had been pissing in the bucket were in on it ...

Some of the food we were getting served up was getting worse; after every meal the swillbins were always overflowing. Our colonel was reputed to have a pig farm and it was said he had the fattest pigs in the country. One of our wags suggested that the swillbins were the only bins in the world to have ulcers. On one occasion someone had shouted across the cookhouse that the cooks were cunts.

'Who called the cooks cunts?' asked the orderly officer.

'Who called the cunts cooks?' shouted someone else.

One day thirty-three of us were called in to the education centre to do a test for the third-class certificate of education. The education certificate was timed in all subjects; an education officer sat at a desk and timed you on each subject. I always thought I was not very attentive at school but something must have sunk in. About a fortnight later the battery orders board carried the results of the examination – I had passed! I don't know how the other thirty-two candidates got on (men and women) but the BSM had got all the results in the battery office. When he addressed us on parade he referred to us as 'semi-educated monkeys'.

Darkie Glover and his mate Miles were the very best of friends and shared everything. Miles had done something wrong and one of the bombardiers had sent Darkie to supervise Miles in cutting the football field with a hand lawnmower, telling Darkie that he may possibly be in with a chance of a stripe. Miles had said to Darkie that if he took a stripe they would not be able to drink in the same bar, and that Darkie would have to drink with the NCOs in their bar. We went to the football field to have a game of football. Darkie was having a sleep on the grass while Miles was swinging the lawn mower round and round his head and passing it from one hand to the other. They had fallen out and every time Darkie passed Miles he would say to him, in a mocking voice, 'Hey,

Milesy, aren't you speaking to your little pudding?' which gave us all a laugh.

The biggest laugh came when we had a brigadier come to inspect us and the camp. It was always a mad rush to get all the billets clean, although they were always spotless, and it was more panic among the senior ranks. Darkie and Miles (as I said) shared everything but they had fallen out. When the Brigadier came inspecting our billet he came to Darkie Glover's bedspace, and stood bemused looking at Darkie's kit – half a block of soap, half a block of blanco, two bits of a safety razor, a bottle with some brasso in it, half a tin of boot polish.

'What is this?' asked the Brigadier.

'Well,' said Darkie, 'me and that cunt opposite have fallen out, and as we share all our cleaning materials we have cut everything in half.'

This seemed to amuse the Brigadier … to think that anyone would have the audacity to tell this to a brigadier.

'Why have you fallen out?' he asked.

'Because he thinks I am going to get a stripe, and that I won't be his mate any more', said Darkie. 'Beside that he has no sense of humour,'

'Why is that?' asked the Brigadier.

'Well, sir, I told him that my brother had been sent to jail for "Black Rape".'

'Black rape,' said the Brigadier, 'what is that?'

'Well, sir, I told him that my brother had been caught shagging a bag of soot but he couldn't see the funny side.'

The Brigadier walked on shaking his head. When he got round to Miles it was the same, half this, half that. 'If you had a girlfriend and you shared her, would you cut her in half?' asked the Brigadier.

'I wouldn't, sir, but that cunt would,' said Miles.
What a bollocking they got from the RSM … taking the piss out of the Brigadier, he said. But the RSM did have a sense of humour, otherwise their feet wouldn't have touched the ground again.

Gunner Marwood had gone to the MO with stomach pains. 'Have you had a bowel movement this morning?' asked the MO.

'Don't know what that is,' said Marwood.

'Are you regular?' asked the MO.

'No I'm a national serviceman,' said Marwood.

'I didn't mean are you a regular soldier, I meant are you regular with your bowel movement? Are you constipated?

'I'm afraid I don't understand,' said Marwood.

'Okay,' said the MO, 'I'll put it in plain English ... Have you shit?'

'No, sir,' said Marwood, 'I thought that was you.'

Chapter XX

The Firing Camp at Sennybridge

OUR FIRST FIRING CAMP WITH THE 3.7 GUN was at Sennybridge in the Brecon Beacons, Wales. We travelled in convoy taking our guns with us ... no women at this camp because we didn't need radar operators for a field shoot. This would be the last one for Bombardier Nicholls, who would be leaving us after this camp. Bombardier Gillespie had already left us and married a nice young WRAC called Rita ... most of the other intake before us had left, which was to prove very interesting and in my case dangerous.

Our first shoot went off well. When we did our next shoot Bdr Nicholls set up all the tannoy stations behind each gun. The tannoys were two-way, one being a loudspeaker for when you gave orders to the guns. When you pressed the button on the top of the tannoy the gunnery sergeant could talk back to repeat the orders given to him ... every order had to be repeated back. I went out with the officer who was taking the shoot and his assistant, TARA (Technical Assistant Royal Artillery). We had just recently been sent a new intake before coming to camp, and these new lads had formed X Troop. The TARA was one of them, called Mick Ayres, a very nice lad, an all-round sportsman, and very brainy. He was assisting Lt Chappel. We were dropped off well in front of the guns with all our equipment. The officer and TARA set up a theodolite instrument to work out our target. I had got into a trench which at some time had been made ready for shoots such as this. It had a bench on which to sit, and a small platform in front of the bench on which to set up the 22 set, place maps etc. There were four corner posts of wood with corrugated tin sheets on top as a roof. When you were sat in the trench you were just head and shoulders above the top, so you could see the target.

Bombardier Nicholls gave out his netting call at the arranged time ... I netted him in loud and clear. What a very good reception here in the Beacons, strength niner. I had a writing pad strapped to my knee as all orders given had to be written down, so if anyone made a mistake it was known which radio operator had made it. The officer and Mick Ayres got into the trench along with another young officer who was learning how to do a shoot. 'Ready,' said Lt Chappel. I opened up:

'Hello Tare Uncle Baker Two Wun. FIRE ORDERS! FIRE ORDERS! FIRE ORDERS! OVER.'

Bombardier Nicholls: 'Hello Tare Uncle Baker Two Wun Battery. Ready, Over.'

'Hello Tare Uncle Baker Two Wun ... Mike target H.E. 117. Mike Oblique Stroke Roger Seven Sixer Fiyve Fower Niner Wun ... Height Wun Niner Hundred Feet ... Oboe Tate Fower Five degrees. Right Ranging. FIRE. OVER'

Every order given had been repeated. The gun on the right of the battery would fire a ranging shot ... we heard the shell go over our heads before we heard the bang of the gun (shell travelling faster than sound). They would report, 'Shot one, Over.' We replied, 'Shot Wun, Out.'

Corrections were then given: add ... go left ... go right ... drop. The ranging gun would fire a shot after every correction until they landed on the selected target (Mike Oblique Stroke Roger = Map Reference ... Oboe Tate = On Target ... H.E. = High Explosive ... Roger = Message received and fully understood ... Wilco = Will Comply to orders given).

When the ranging gun was on target all other guns were put on the same bearing and a fuse setting was given. The fuse could be set by hand with a fuse key, or set by the gun automatically if under control of the radar system. The order was then given: Ten Rounds Gunfire, Fire, Over. When all guns had fired ten rounds they would report: Shot, Over. We replied: Shot, Out. While all these rounds were passing over our heads, there was a shellburst very near to us so we all got down low in the hole as metal rattled on the corrugated sheets above us – shrapnel! 'Cease Fire!' I shouted into the mike. Lt Chappel looked at the writing pad on my knee. It wasn't us who had set a short fuse. He told the guns to stand down: 'Hellow Tare Uncle Baker Two Wun, Target Destroyed, Record as target Able Wun Wun Zero One, Battery stand down, Over.'

When we got back the Bombardier's pad was looked at. He was correct so it wasn't the radio operators. Although Lt Chappel swore and cursed, no one had made the blunder. Which man on the ammunition had set the wrong fuse? Which gun had it been fired from? It could have been very serious for us out in front, but we were lucky.

Bombardier Nicholls came to all his signallers afterwards and said we had been congratulated by some 'top brass' on the clarity of our radio net, and of the precise and clear speech of the orders passed during the shoot.

Soon after we arrived back, Bombardier Nicholls left us; all the signals team were sorry to see him go. He had been held in high esteem by all of us for his excellence as an instructor and as a very humane leader. Soon after this I was promoted to full Bombardier and put in charge of a barrack room of the new X Troop, a grand set of lads. Gunner Rhodes from York, Gunner Parkin from Scholes, Mick Ayres, to name but a few. I was now also in charge of the signals team, so not only did I have the inventory of equipment on my signature but also a barrack room.

When the barrack room was handed over to me I refused to sign for it because there was a bed missing. BSM Stamp said, 'Come on, get the fucking inventory signed.' But I stuck out until another inventory was printed without the missing bed.

I was also now eligible for guard commander duties, because bombardiers were now doing sergeants' duties, the sergeants mostly being married. At Hobbs Barracks we only did a twelve-hour guard (unless it was at Shirley Park). When you had done guard commander at night you were on duty the following day as ROS (Regimental Orderly Sergeant). The Regimental Police did the day duties at the main gate, with Bombardier Head in charge of them – he had a very bad reputation for nastiness towards any prisoners in the guard room cells.

Chapter XXI

Hobbs Barracks and More of the Happenings

I HAD TAKEN OVER FROM THE REGIMENTAL POLICE as guard commander for the night. Bdr Head said that there was a prisoner in the cells.
'Watch him,' he said. 'He's built like a brick wall and can be very violent.'
After a while I went to check on the prisoner, and looked at him in disbelief,
for he had been in my home on many occasions! My father was a railway
engine driver and this lad had been his fireman. He was Gunner Wood
who had deserted before my intake and lived in Brighouse, Yorkshire, not
very far from my home. He was built like a brick wall ... but violent, no.

Later on in the evening I gave him some supper, something that he
didn't normally get. The Regimental Police lived in a block of cells at one
side of the guardroom, the prisoners in cells at the other side. At about
2200 hours Bombardier Head come out of his quarters into the guard
room, took the keys for the cells from the glass case on the wall and brought
Woody from his cell. I asked him what he was doing, and he said that he
was going to have Woody scrub the floor.

'Get him back in his cell,' I said.

'No,' he said, 'he's going to scrub the floor.'

'If you persist,' I said, 'I will place you in a cell for disobeying an order
from the guard commander.'

'I am in charge of this guardroom,' he said

'Yes, you were until I relived you at 1800 hours. Now I am in charge
until 0600, so hurry up and piss off,' I said.

He was going to report me to the RSM, so I challenged him to do so.
He said he was senior to me in rank as he had been a bombardier a lot
longer than I had. So I told him to do the duty of the Regimental Orderly
Sergeant the following day, a duty that we had to do after doing guard
commander.

I took the sick and defaulters parade in the morning, then went to meet
the orderly officer to accompany him on his rounds of the cookhouse. We
came to one table after another and asked if there were any complaints
about the food, but there were no complaints – no one ever did complain

about the breakfasts. At dinner time I met the orderly officer again. Going round the tables, he asked if there were any complaints. One young woman said, 'Yes sir, what we want is longer tools and shorter periods.'

'I beg your pardon,' he said.

'She's having a joke, sir,' I said.

'Not in very good taste,' he said.

At another table a lad complained that he couldn't lift his cabbage … it kept coming up in one big piece as he picked it up with his fork. The officer had a good look at the so-called cabbage, which was found to be a net dishcloth having been dyed green in the vat of cabbage. The explanation given by the cook sergeant was that it must have fallen from the side of the sink as the cabbage was getting washed.

After the orderly officer had gone, I sat down to dinner with Charlie Gladys and a few more mates. Trudy Swan, a very small girl who worked in the cookhouse, came over to where we were sitting. 'What's wanking?' she asked. I said there was a place in China called Wanking. Charlie told her that when she went across to the Regimental Butcher for the cookhouse meat rations, she should ask Butch Devaney … we all knew that Butch was a great joker. 'Oh yes,' said Charlie, 'Butch will tell her.'

When I met the orderly officer for the evening meal he went to the row of hotplates to have a look what was being served up. Looking in to one of the big oblong tins he asked one of the women what it was. She was called 'Big Elsie' (I didn't know her surname). 'What is it?' she repeated. 'It's Hot Cock and Bollock roll, with Spotted Dick for afters.'

The officer's face went crimson. 'What did she say?' he asked me.

'Oh! She's always like that, sir,' I said, 'always ready to have a joke with the lads. Says things like that to everyone who asks her.'

'Goodness me,' he said, 'I would not like to be married to a foul-mouthed bitch like that, just imagine waking up in the morning and finding her at you side.'

It was not unusual the things she said. Every time I was on ROS duties, it was the same. Most of the different orderly officers that we had knew 'Big Elsie'.

About a week after Trudy Swan had asked her question, I was told to call in to see the Battery Commander, as was Charlie Gladys. We were asked about what we had said to Trudy Swan in regard to her question about wanking. I told him just what I had said and Charlie told what he had said. 'You two are a couple of fucking idiots,' he said and gave us a right good bollocking. But he couldn't hide his mirth and then told us that the BSM had put Butch Devaney on a charge for indecent exposure. It seemed that Trudy had gone to the Butcher's stores for the meat on that particular day. Whilst waiting she had told Butch that she had asked Bombardier Barraclough and Charlie Gladys what was the meaning of the word wanking, and that Charlie had told her that she could find out from Butch. The story went that Butch had got his dick out and told Trudy to get hold of it; she had run out of the place screaming.

Butch came up in front of the Battery Commander on a charge. Two lance bombardiers were his escort and the BSM marched them in to the office. When asked for his explanation, Butch told his version. To satisfy the women officers on the camp Butch was given fourteen days CB (confined to barracks) which meant that every evening for fourteen days he would have to be on guard mounting parade in full FSMO and his kit would have to be up to a very high standard. As he was the Regimental Butcher no one had ever bothered him about his kit, because he spent most of his time seeing to the meat. All the time he was mounting with the guard other lads lent him items of their kit because his was such a shambles. In the NAAFI during the evening Butch would give his account of what had been read from the charge sheet ... His version was: 2239???? Gunner Devaney. To the prejudice of Good Order and Military Discipline you did on the said date whip out your prick and tell a member of the Women's Royal Army Corps to grab a hold of it. What have you got to say? Guilty, sir ... That was Butch's account. Poor Trudy, she got plenty of stick from both the men and women. When Trudy passed many of them they would shout, 'Hey, Trudy, did he have a big-un?'

Chapter XXII

The Manoeuvres in Lingfield – The Coal Detail – Lingfield Bonfire Night and Other Events

WE WERE DOING A SCHEME in the village of Lingfield ... two forces attacking each other (as though German Paratroops had landed). We were all quite enjoying it when suddenly we were called in halfway through the exercise. It was announced that the King had passed away. For reasons that I didn't understand, some of the Scots lads cheered and were singing 'At the end of the day just kneel and say Poor Old George passed away today.' The ones singing were in a minority and it was only on the intervention of a senior NCO that the mock battle we were doing didn't turn into a real one. All our officers were walking around in black suits and black bowler hats, one lad was overheard to say, 'Don't they look a lot of cunts.'

The coal detail was another job we had to do. A bombardier would take two men to the coal yard behind the NAAFI and fill up about two tons of coal in one hundredweight sacks. We would then load it onto a civilian lorry and take it out to Married Quarters, which were a few miles from the camp. On one of these coal details I was in the cab of this dilapidated old lorry; my two men were on the back. We were going down a steep hill at a terrific rate of knots. The men were shouting for the driver to slow down, while I was bracing myself for a crash and asking the driver if his brakes had failed. 'No, I always give it some stick,' he said. 'I'm used to going at great speeds and I get to the top of the next hill very easy.'

'Well slow down when I'm with you,' I said. It turned out that he was a civilian pilot, and helped his father (who owned the haulage business) when he had some spare time.

The people of Lingfield celebrated bonfire night very enthusiastically. One bonfire night they invited the entire 46th to attend, at which the people gave us a very good time. All the villagers were dressed in the clothes of that period (Gunpowder Plot), the food was good and we thoroughly enjoyed the hospitality. One man asked me if I knew who was the best man ever to get into parliament. 'Winston Churchill,' I said (I was a great admirer of Winston Churchill). 'Wrong,' said the man, 'it was Guy Fawkes.'

I was taken into a military hospital somewhere near Forest Row with a very badly swollen arm, where I was told that it was an infected mosquito bite and was all gathering near my elbow. I was laid in bed when a medical orderly came in and had a look at the swelling. Suddenly he bent my arm at the elbow which caused the swelling to burst. The pus spurted out of my arm and sprayed the low ceiling. It was the only time in my life that I ever passed out; it was a feeling like all the blood was draining from my body.

Chapter XXIII

New Officer in Signals Team –
The Antics of a Cab-happy Officer –
A Day to be Proud of During my Service

A COUPLE OF YOUNG OFFICERS HAD BEEN COMING into the signals
class who joined in the training, learning the phonetic alphabet and
all the radio procedure. They along with the other lads were taught how
to use their voice over the air ... RSVP = Rhythm Speed Volume Pitch
... never to use foul language over the air, and always to stick to the codes
given, i.e. ours was TUB = Tare Uncle Baker. After they had gained a little
knowledge of radio procedure they came with us out into the field on
schemes. One of them went with my team and the other went with another
team. When they got on the air their procedure was nothing like what
they had been taught – they didn't use the codes, they swore ... It mattered
not how much I told them, they still went on calling each other by their
Christian names, having conversations about what they had done over the
weekend in their posh plum-in-the-mouth speech. When I pulled them
up, I was told that they were officers and I couldn't tell them what to do.
It was a case of don't tell your betters what to do even though many of
these young officers had no experience of life beyond their own privileged
circle. As far as they were concerned we were the peasants, but they had
to pick our brains to gain knowledge of army life. There were some very
decent young officers who had probably been in cadet forces at their
universities, and did have good knowledge.

One of the two officers got himself placed as Signals Officer, and much
to my delight he wanted all the signals equipment on his signature. I
checked all the equipment with him in the signals stores and he signed the
inventory. It was now off my mind. I now had only a barrack room and
its contents on my charge.

One afternoon the new Signals Officer told me that we would be going
out early the next morning on a field telephone/cable laying scheme. I
asked him if I should load the necessary equipment onto the 15 cwt Bedford

truck. 'No,' he said, 'I will bring it all, get an early breakfast and meet me by the signals stores with your men.'

Ashdown Forest ... he sent me off in one direction with two men, after I had joined the loose ends of two drums of Don-eight cable with a semi-permanent joint. Reeling out the cable as we went, he shouted that he would give me a ring when we got connected at the other end. They then went on their way reeling out their cable. Eventually we connected our Tele 'L' (field telephone) to the end of our wire and proceeded to do a Click and Blow test = pressing the pressel switch and blowing into the phone. Nothing ... test the terminals = putting a coin between the wired-up terminals and winding the cranking handle to give you a slight electric shock. Nothing. On lifting the lid on the case we looked inside – no batteries. We just sat down and waited. The officer followed our wire and came ranting and raging.

'Bombardier, why the facking hell don't you answer you phone? I have been cranking like fack and getting no answer, are you facking incompetent or what?'

'Did I not teach you the click and blow test? Did I not teach you the terminal shock test? And who got all the equipment out this morning?' I asked.

'Yes I do know all the tests,' he said.

'Did you do the tests before you phoned us?'

'Yes I did,' he said.

'Well why didn't you notice that there were no batteries in the phones, or why didn't you put some in when you loaded up?' His face went red. 'I wonder what the RSM will say when I tell him that I have been accused of incompetence,' I said. I wouldn't have said anything to the RSM but I certainly put the breeze up the officer who couldn't apologise enough.

There was a big hospital in East Grinstead, Queen Elizabeth Hospital. This was where plastic surgery was done on the gallant aircrews who had been badly burned and maimed during the War. Some of these men had artificial limbs; many could use the limbs to attach a knife and fork or any tools they needed to use; some were in wheel chairs. They were invited to come to Hobbs Barracks and spend the day with us. We entertained them with visits to all our guns, radar and generator sites, showing them how everything was operated. All of them of course were very well used to radio procedures, and were very interested in the 22 sets. One chap who had been shot down in the Battle of Britain got talking to me about a set he had built himself whilst convalescing in the hospital. He said he was a radio ham and had probably listened in to us transmitting because he said he sometimes tuned in to military wavebands as he was searching the air waves. The war hero had artificial hands but could use them brilliantly. They enjoyed their day with us and the food provided because it had been specially prepared for them. These were some of the 'Few'; these were MEN. I think to have actually met some of them was a great honour and I felt very proud. When these men were defending us I was about ten years old.

Gunner Rhodes was from York, a member of X Troop. He was also a bit of a comic and had been posted to the MT section as a driver of 15 cwt Bedford trucks. We had one officer (no name) who wore bottle bottom glasses and was 'cab happy' – any vehicle left standing without a driver, and he was into the cab. Driving instruction could be had if you could get an officer to sign the 'Work Ticket'. This officer would sign a work ticket anytime, providing that he was included with the learners. We would go out in the truck without the canvas canopy which enabled those in the back to see what was going on in the cab. The officer was desperate to get a driving licence. I believe he had said that his father would buy him a sports car if he ever got a licence.

The officer had started a cycling club but were not allowed to ride within the camp, so they had to wheel their bikes out of the camp, and when they arrived back, dismount at the gate and wheel them up the camp. If they saw our 'cab-happy' officer behind the wheel of a vehicle they would pretend to scatter and take the piss out of him. One day Gunner Shone must have forgotten something and returned to the barrack room, leaving his Matador (gun tractor) outside with the engine running. 'Oh my god,' someone shouted to Gunner Shone, 'your vehicle is running away.' We all dashed out of the room into the road just in time to see the Matador turn the corner at the bottom of the camp.

'Someone must be driving it,' shouted Tommy Bestwick, another driver. We took a short cut between the billets to get onto the road which ran up the camp. Happy as a lark was 'Cab Happy', driving this very heavy vehicle.

'Fucking hell,' shouted Ron Jones, 'it's Cab Happy.'

A group of officers, who had been out of camp, were wheeling their bicycles up the camp. 'Fuck Me,' shouted an officer, 'Lt ???? is driving a

Matador.' To take the piss out of him, they all threw their bikes down and jumped over the fence into the Colonel's garden. To take the piss out of them, he drove straight at them grinning like a Cheshire cat, but he lost control and was doing well over the five-mile-per-hour limit; he ran over four bikes, bending them beyond recognition, ran through the Colonel's fence, and if he hadn't stalled the engine as he sank the wheels into the lawn there could have been fatalities.

I don't know to this day what the outcome of that incident was, but some weeks later we were out again in the Bedford truck. 'Cab Happy was saying he was bored because it wasn't his turn to have a drive so Gunner Rhodes said to him, 'Do you want to read some of the letters I have got from my Old Tart?' and he reached into his inside pocket. 'Don't you have a girlfriend?' asked Rhodes.

'No, I don't know much about girls,' said Cab Happy.

Gunner Rhodes then said to him, 'Do you mean to tell me that you've never felt a cunt.'

'Oh yes,' said Cab Happy, 'I felt a right cunt when I went through the Colonel's fence.'

One of our X Troop lads had got a very greasy pair of boots. I even tried to get them shiny but to no avail. The troop officer was going to put him on a charge but I told the officer it wasn't the lad's fault because the leather was very greasy. 'Right,' said the officer, 'send him up to my quarters and I will give him some methylated spirits.' He saw me look puzzled, then he said, 'Why would I have methylated spirits? Because I drink the stuff.' No wonder he had a very yellow complexion. It was a revelation to me as I never knew that anyone could drink meths.

I had another run in with Bombardier Head. Gunner Jenkins (Regimental Police) had been told to supervise the prisoner, Woody, who I saw cutting grass with a jackknife; he was getting tufts of grass in one hand and cutting them. I walked down to the guard room, and told Bdr Head to get Woody a lawn mower or take him back to his cell. It would have been no use me getting on to Gunner Jenkins, who was a very nice friendly lad, but was under orders from Bdr Head. 'Fuck off and mind your own fucking business, or I'll report you to the RSM for interfering in Regimental Police affairs.'

'Okay, let's both go to the RSM's office, and we'll tell him that you have been depriving the prisoner of his three cigarettes a day ration,' I said

(Woody had told me about it, so I had been getting some of the lads to put fags under his door). The challenge was enough to make Bdr Head back down. Some time after that Woody was taken for court martial and I never saw him again. Although I have lived within a few miles of his home town all my life, I have never encountered him. I remember him telling me that if ever he met Bdr Head in civilian life, he would wring his neck.

Chapter XXIV

Throw Their Kit out of the Window

X TROOP HAD BEEN OUT ON A SCHEME and had then finished off by charging over the assault course; normally water bottles were never filled or used but the troop officer wanted them filled.

We returned to the billets in the late afternoon, the officer having told everyone to empty and wash out their water bottles, get a shower then go for tea. We had been dressed in battle order, everyone threw their webbing on the lockers at the side of their beds, then as they got showered and off to the cookhouse, the officer returned.

'Have they all emptied and washed out their water bottles?' he asked me.

'Yes sir, as far as I know they have,' I replied.

'Let's walk round the room and check them,' he said. So we walked round the room and he found three water bottles still full. He pulled the stopper from each bottle as he found them and poured the contents over the kit of the offenders, wetting everything including the bedding.

'Open the window, Bombardier,' he said. I opened the window. 'Now throw all their kit out,' he said.

'Can't do that, sir,' I said.

'Do as you are facking well told and don't tell me what I can and can't do,' he said.

'KRRs [Kings Rules and Regulations] state that a man's kit can only be thrown on the bed,' I told him. I didn't know if that was true but I had heard it somewhere.

He then went ahead and threw all their kit out himself, at the same time calling me a facking barrack room lawyer. The men concerned returned from the cookhouse, and after a tirade of the foulest language refused point blank to retrieve their kit.

Out on parade next morning three men were minus belts and gaiters. When asked where their equipment was, they said it was where the troop officer had thrown it, and it would remain there until the officer put it back.

The officer duly arrived to take over the inspection from the Sergeant, and was told what had transpired.

'Go get your kit,' he told the three men.

'No sir,' they said, 'you threw it out, you return it.'

The Sergeant took the officer to one side and must have told him that it was against regulations to throw men's kit out of windows, so the officer backed down and retrieved the kit, the look on his face suggesting that he would give them a hard time at a later date.

Chapter XXV

Firing Camp at Towen – Richard Dimbleby's Visit

T owen, merionethshire, our last firing camp. We were camped in a large field in the shadow of Cader Idris, a mountain of about 2,000 feet. The 4.5s were situated on the coast overlooking Cardigan Bay. Here at this camp we had to collect our own ammunition from a dump near some railway sidings; the 28lb shells were in long wooden boxes and with the box they probably weighed about 40lb. We were throwing the boxes from a railway truck onto the lorry as though they were nothing, so we must have all been very fit, but we fell foul of a Sergeant Major who was in charge of the ammunition. 'You fucking ignorant morons,' he screamed at us. 'Throwing the boxes of ammunition about like that, are you trying to blow up the whole fucking place; have you got a grudge against the Welsh?' he went on. We were reported to our commander who barred us from going near the place again.

On the gunsite, there were big cauldrons of water which had a fire underneath them. The water was boiling and after a shoot the empty shell cases had to be boiled out and the used primer removed. We had done misfire drill on many occasions ... if a shell failed to go off when struck by the firing pin, permission was asked from 'Fire Control' for permission to recock the gun and fire again. The procedure was that if the shell failed to go off a second time, Control would give the order to unload. One of the men feeding up the shells would get a winding handle, fit the handle onto the bottom of the firing tray and wind it up. Doing this sent a stopper to the top of the tray. When the breach was opened the shell would rest against the stopper; the shell was then slowly wound down to the bottom of the tray before being lifted out and handed to a man who would carry it to the rear of the gun and place it a safe distance from the other ammunition.

I had trained as a gunner but I had never been on a gun firing live ammunition. This would be my last chance. I had got all the communications working nicely ready for the shoot so I went and told our firing officer that I would like the opportunity to do a job I had been trained for. He said okay and to go on No. 1 gun as layer for elevation.

When the shoot commenced I was amazed that I hardly heard the bang from the gun I was sat on, whereas the gun next to us was deafening. We had 'blacked out and matched up' the dials to correspond with the radar instructions. When we were matched with the dials we would shout, 'On QE [Quadrant elevation]. On Fuse. On Bearing.' Firing then started. Behind the shield on the 4.5 we couldn't see our target which was a sleeve towed by a Beaufighter. We were banging away nicely when suddenly the call came, 'No. 1 misfire.' How lucky can you get – my first live shoot and we get a misfire! The SMIG (Sergeant Major Instructor of Gunnery), or as we called them Ack I Gee, shouted through the tannoy, 'No. 1 Misfire, permission to recock and fire again.'

Okay, came the reply from Control to try again. The rammer was placed in position to hold the shell while the gun was recocked ... the lever beach mechanism was opened and closed again ... No. 5 on the gun slapped the 'Pig's ear' (firing lever). Nothing.

'No. 1 Misfire. Stand by to unload,' said Control.

'Right lads,' shouted the SMIG. 'I know that you arseholes have started to bubble, but don't panic. You know the drill for unloading.'

We had been told by our gunnery instructors that on some misfires all the men had backed away from the gun when the order to unload had been given. On one occasion a SMIG had been stood behind the gun and had been killed when the breach block had hit him in the chest. What nice thoughts ...

'Unload,' came the order from Control. Everybody did as they should, but as the breach was slowly opened (probably only a fraction of an inch) 'Boom', it went off. The lad opening the breach caught the main blast. I was sat below him and caught some of it and the lad on the ammunition tray did too. No one was badly hurt but the blast of cordite had peppered us ... it was all down my back. The lad who got the worst was covered all down his front, being peppered all yellow, face, hands, all his belt and clothes. It was a good thing he was wearing a steel helmet or his hair would have burned.

The SMIG congratulated us on remaining calm, saying that he hoped none of us had got 'brown underpants', jokingly admitting that he had 'shit myself'.

The campsite was separated from the sea by a fairly high bank of pebbles; to get to the beach we had to cross a railway line and climb up the banking.

Every chance we got we were in the sea swimming, while at other times we would go up Cader Idris.

One night there was a freak storm. The sea came right over the banking and flooded the whole campsite ... the tents were awash ... duckboards were floating ... what a mess we were in. Richard Dimbleby was doing a programme at that time called Down Your Way and here he was visiting us. The Artificer Sergeant (Tiffy) was trying to get a pump going to get rid of some water, the language he was using being abominable. I didn't think that Richard Dimbleby would be broadcasting it.

The Quartermaster was up to his waist in water, and was moving his stores onto some higher ground. He wanted his telephone moving so I told him that the phone was a civilian one, and if he got permission from the local exchange I would move it for him. I also told him that if they gave permission, I would have to speak to them. He phoned the exchange and explained what he wanted. Okay, go ahead, they said. He then told them that I wanted a word and passed the phone over to me. I told them what I was about to do and requested that as their switchboard was the ancient

Just been swimming in Cardigan Bay. Back row, L–R: *Tommy Bestwick; Gnr Evans; Bdr Barraclough.* Front row: *Ron Jones (kneeling).*

81

type with a crank generator, not to crank our number, adding that I would ring them. I disconnected the wiring and led it to the higher ground. I climbed up the pole on the end of the marquee, and put a double-barrel hitch over the top of the pole ready now to connect the bare wires to the phone inside the marquee. Someone cranked the generator at the exchange. I don't know what voltage I was hit by but I was thrown off the top of the marquee. I was very lucky I wasn't standing in water. When I phoned the exchange to tell them I had completed the job I gave them a right roasting. They thought they had got a lunatic on the line, having changed shifts and knew nothing about the line change.

All in all we had a very good time at Towen (Tywen). Our NAAFI was a big marquee, and I will say that wherever soldiers went we could rely on the NAAFI.

On our last night we sat and told jokes, and had a bit of a sing-song. Gunner Joe Fellows, a Londoner, gave us his rendition of 'My Old Man's a Dustman'. I can still remember the words, even though I only heard it once:

My old man's a dustman, he wears a dustman's hat,
He killed ten thousand Germans, what do you think of that.
One lay here, one lay there, one lay round the corner,
One poor soul with a bullet up his hole was crying out for water.
Water! Water! Water came at last but I don't want your water you can stick it up your arse.
Oh bread and cheese and all his families if you don't come quick
I'll tickle your prick with a bunch of celeree.

Imagine that sung in Joe's cockney accent. Another lad got up and gave some wartime poetry:

If it wasn't for Hitler the fish wouldn't be getting littler
If it wasn't for Hess chips wouldn't be getting less
If it wasn't for Goering we'd be getting more in.

Followed by:

Land of dope and stories now no longer free
How can we console thee short of meat and tea

Tighter still and tighter shall thy belt be set
Strachy made the hungry, Cripps thy money shall get.

Strachy at the time was Minister of Food. Cripps was Chancellor of the Exchequer. He then finished off with one I don't quite remember, but is was something like:

Stafford Cripps, Stafford Cripps, lend me you grey mare
All along out along Clement Attlee
Ernest Bevin, ????? ????? ?????
Old Uncle Nanny Shinwell and all, Old Uncle Nanny Shinwell and all.

These were all politicians of the day.

Back to Lingfield and very soon (a couple of months) DEMOB.

One of our jokers would make a point of getting a little way behind any of the women NCOs and would shout 'Cunt'. When the NCO spun round he would carry on singing 'Cunt tell a waltz from a tango, cunt tell what my feet were going to do, cunt tell a waltz from a tango, even when I danced with you.'

Sometimes he would shout 'Hey', When they turned, he carried on, 'Hey Mambo Mambo Italiano, hey mambo' etc.

On other occasions he would shout 'Here'. Whoever it was in front of him would turn round and he then went on, 'Here we are again, happy as can be, all good pals and jolly good company'. One day a very big WRAC corporal had him by the throat, having had enough of him over a period of time. He said to her that there was no law against singing ... she said she had a law against him 'taking the piss'.

Chapter XXVI

The Assault Course at Hobbs Barracks

THE ASSAULT COURSE RAN THE FULL LENGTH OF THE CAMP and was in the woods to the left of the one-way system. We had taken X troop there for the first time along with two young officers. At the start there was a long oblong pit, 3 feet wide and about 15 feet long. About 3 feet up the length of the pit there was a plank across the pit. When you ran towards the pit you had to jump over the plank, which then landed you in deep muddy water; if you landed on this side of the plank it was only a foot.

Gunner Ashley couldn't clear the plank (or wouldn't). When you landed in the deep part you had to keep your rifle above your head. We had all done it except Ashley. It was bitterly cold and all the lads wanted to get on with it, so they kidded Ashley by moving the plank back a bit. He then cleared the plank, slipped on the edge of the shallow bit and disappeared into the deep part rifle and all. He came up with muddy water running out of his very blonde hair, digging his nails into the slippery bank, looking like a mad Rhino and minus his rifle. He set off running through the wood towards the barracks, and wouldn't stop however much we called him to come back, but just shouted, 'I'll get even with all you lousy bastards.'

The next obstacle was a hole in the ground which was also full of muddy water. You had to throw your rifle, butt first and land it about six feet in front of you. Then you got down the hole head first, swam through an earthenware pipe and climbed out of the hole at the other end, picking up your rifle and carrying on to the next obstacle. Gunner Huttle was very big and as we were in battle order the pack on his shoulders made him bigger. He had gone head first into the pipe but didn't seem to be moving. One of the sergeants was shouting (in a jocular way), 'Come on you big fat cunt, come on you fucking bladder of lard.' Bubbles were coming to the surface as the sergeant realised that something was wrong, so we got Huttle by the feet and dragged him out – good job we did as his pack had got stuck and he couldn't go one way or the other. When I look back these water obstacles must have been terrifying to the non-swimmers.

Bombardier Barraclough.

The next obstacle was a very high wall, where six men would form a ladder with their rifles and the rest of the men would run up and clear the wall, the last lot pulling each other up. Then came a long wide board suspended at each corner on a cable; you ran across this as it swung about, most of us falling over. After that came thickets of brambles and hawthorns, and then 'The Tree'. This very tall tree had 'step irons', in order to get onto a narrow platform which had been built around the trunk about 15 feet up ... when you got onto the platform, and having first strapped your rifle across you shoulders, you jumped out into midair and grabbed a rope which was hanging about 5 feet away from you, gripped the rope and went down hand over hand (if you slid your hands down the rope you got rope burns). We had all completed this, many having splashed down into the sloppy mud, when Sgt Russell invited the two officers to have a go at this obstacles because they had stood back. 'Come on, sirs,' he said 'you have done okay up to now.' One of them climbed up and after a few times leaning forward and hesitating he managed to do it. 'Come on and have a go, it's not too bad,' he told the other officers.

The other officer said, 'Not facking likely. If I had been meant to fly I would have had wings.' It was pointed out to him that he would never be able to ask his men to do something that he couldn't do himself. There was also a lot of clucking and calls of 'Chicken'. Reluctantly he climbed up, and after a lot of jeering and egging him on he finally dived for the rope ... 'Splat', it was the best swallow dive I ever did see, straight down into the slop ... rifle sling too slack, hitting him on the back of his head.

The last obstacle on the course was a long stretch of barbed wire suspended about 18 inches above the ground; you had to crawl underneath it doing what was called the 'monkey crawl'. Sgt Brittain was sat behind a Bren gun and it was set on a tripod. He explained that the gun was on 'fixed lines' – when it was fired it would send a stream of bullets along the top of the wire to ensure that you kept absolutely flat on the ground. Battle initiation, he called it.

'When you go under the wire I will keep firing a burst,' he said. 'Oh, by the way, Huttle, if you get your big fat arse up in the air, the stream of bullets will plough a furrow across it.' We found out afterwards that he was kidding – he was only firing blanks!

Sgt Russell then threw a phosphorous grenade right into the brambles and hawthorns as a demonstration; some of us were detailed to stay behind and put out the fires.

Looking forward to a nice hot shower, we made our way back to the billets, only to find the officers and sergeants there and wanting to use our showers. But there wasn't any hot water as all the taps had been turned on and left on, officers quarters included. Gunner Ashley was sat on his bed smirking – after he had legged it he had been round running all the hot water off.

They say that he who laughs last laughs longest. Ashley was made to get back into his wet clothes, was taken into the wood and told to get his rifle from the pit. Get spotlessly clean or face a nice spell in military detention … it was only the fact that he hadn't been in the Army very long that saved him from detention.

One man who had a very long service (wore a lot of stripes upside down on his sleeve) had gone to London for the weekend. He had met up with another soldier who had asked for the loan of a shilling, saying he had lost his money and couldn't afford a bed for the night. Our man told him that he didn't have a lot of money, but if he wanted he could share his bed in the Union Jack Club. During the night the Military Police had gone into the club and found them in the same bed … the charge was 'Gross Indecency'. It was a very grave offence in the Army. Our man usually played the drums for the Salvation Army on a Sunday morning. On his demob he was going to get a job with the Corps of Commissionaires. He was represented at his court martial by lawyers from the Salvation Army (so we were told) and got away with the charge of indecency but was discharged dishonourably for harbouring a deserter.

Gunner Carrol, who had deserted some time during our early days at Hobbs Barracks, had got a job somewhere in London. On his way to work one morning and thinking he was late, he had looked into a car to see the time on the dashboard clock. A policeman thought he was acting suspiciously and collared him. Carrol thought he had been caught for desertion and admitted that he was in fact a deserter.

Chapter XXVII

The Raid on the Armoury –
Women with the .303 Rifle –
More Happenings at Hobbs Barracks

THERE HAD BEEN A RAID at the REME Depot at Arborfield, Nr Reading, so we were put on full alert as the sentries at Arborfield had been left tied up. It was said that someone was after getting weapons ...

Some weeks later I was guard commander on what turned out to be a very eventful night. First of all, one of my prowler guards came in and said that the lights in one of the boiler houses kept going back on whenever he switched them off. Then he said that one of the barrack rooms still had the light on and wouldn't put them off.

I left the guard room to my second in command and went up the camp with the prowler. Coming to the boiler house in question, the lights were on. I opened the door, reached my hand round the corner and switched them off, whereupon a voice shouted, 'Leave the fucking lights alone you stupid bastards.' I went in to find a certain little fat man up the side of the boiler with a certain little WRAC, both stark naked.

'Oh, it's you, Bombardier,' he said, 'I thought it was that prowler guard.'

'Leave the lights off,' I said, 'the orderly officer won't be pleased if she sees any lights on.'

'Oh, fuck the orderly officer,' he said. 'Who's on tonight?'

'Miss Dene, I think,' I replied.

I heard a noise behind me and turned round – it wasn't Miss Dene but another woman officer. She saw the naked man and asked what was going on, fortunately without hearing his remark about the orderly officer; nor could she see the WRAC up the side of the boiler. I'll give him his due, he was a quick thinker, telling her that he had fallen into a pit full of water whilst taking a short cut through the wood, said he had been to the pub, now he was drying his clothes over the boiler.

She was very red faced and didn't question his excuse. 'I was coming down to turn out the guard but I won't bother now,' she said.

I told her that I had come to investigate why the lights were on in the boiler house. We walked her back to her quarters avoiding the hut where the other lights were on. She bid us goodnight and added, 'Have a nice night,' and then said, 'what a sight the little fat man was, he looked like a beetroot which had just been dug up.'

Coming down the camp we came to the hut with the light on ... the prowler guard hammered on the wooden wall with his pickaxe handle shouting, 'Put those lights off now.'

A gruff gravelled voice shouted back, 'Fuck off now or I will come out and kick your fucking head in.'

I then banged on the hut with my fist and shouted, 'Guard Commander, get those lights off now; that's an order.'

The window above us opened and a head popped out; it was Goody. 'Just let me have a couple more hands of cards. I've nearly got all my money back off these cheating bastards in here,' he said.

'Okay, make it quick and get the lights off,' I said.

'Right, thanks, Bombardier,' he said.

I had just got settled down and was having a pot of tea ... 'Halt, who goes there?' I heard the shout, then again, then 'Turn out the guard!' On going outside we found the sentry having problems with two drunken WRACs who were trying to get his rifle from him and generally taking the piss. I asked them to go to their billet peacefully because they should have been in camp by 10.30, but they refused and said that I was playing fucking soldiers. I gave them another chance to change their minds and get to their billets without any more trouble but they carried on taunting the guard and using very foul language, so there was no alternative but to place them under arrest. Into a cell they went, their officer was called and she wasn't very pleased to have been awakened. Both girls were put on a charge.

The ration stores and the armoury were next door to each other in a building constructed of corrugated steel sheets. The back of the building was in the woods on the right side of the camp, the inside of the building being partitioned off, one side of the partition rations, the other side armoury. The very big window at the back covered each side of the partition and was covered by iron bars.

Suddenly we heard the call from across by the armoury, 'Turn out the guard.' It was one of the prowler sentries. We ran over to where he was and he said that someone was in the armoury. We ran through the gap between the buildings to get to the rear of the buildings where shadowy figures could be seen running away. I shouted, 'Halt or I will fire,' then we heard someone shout, 'Keep running, the bastards don't have live ammo.' The police were informed that the intruders had got away in vehicles that had been parked on the road at the other side of the wood. We never heard any more about that incident (looking back from now I have my suspicions about who gave them the information about the armoury). The irony of it was that they got in the wrong half of the building, into the ration stores. What we did prove was that we were alert. What a night it had been!

During the day, after the tour round the cookhouse at breakfast with the orderly officer, I was called to the battery office where the two WRAC troublemakers were on a charge. I had to give my version of events, but never said anything about them trying to get the sentry's rifle from him, nor did I mention the foul language. They both received seven days CB for being out late and causing a nuisance as they came in. Both of them called me a lousy bastard when they passed me later and said they would get their revenge.

When I had been home on my last leave I had met and started going out with an Austrian girl. When I wrote to her it took me ages to compile a letter as she didn't speak any English and I didn't speak German. When I got a letter in return to mine I had to use my English/German dictionary, which took some time. I did manage to acquire a very little knowledge of German this way. Tommy Bestwick from Stoke also had a German girl-friend and now and again I was able to help him a little. My problem was solved when Bombardier Neil Harris joined us from another regiment. He spoke German fluently and was kind enough to interpret my letters for me. Neil didn't have long to do in the Army and said he was joining Customs and Excise when he was demobbed.

I was detailed one day to take the women attached to our troop on a small firing range we had in the camp. It didn't take very long for some of them to become very proficient with the .303 rifle, others proved a big problem.

Private Roberta Pratton, from Bristol, was down getting ready to fire; she was shown how to get her body oblique to the line of fire; how to get the centre of the foresight in the centre of the backsight in the centre of the target, with the sights upright; how to hold the stock with the left hand and the small of the butt with the right. You can teach a person so much. Private

Pratton was gripping the small of the butt with her finger on the trigger and her thumb stuck out, so she was told that if she fired the rifle with her thumb in that position, when the rifle kicked back it would cause her thumbnail to scratch the side of her face. 'Squeeze the trigger, don't jerk it,' I said. She fired, snatching on the trigger, the rifle kicked back because she wasn't holding it firmly into her shoulder and her thumbnail put a nice scratch along her cheek. She jumped up, threw the rifle down and stormed off shouting 'Fuck you Bombardier, fuck your rifles, I'm not firing the fucking things again, they're fucking dangerous.' What a tirade! All the other girls were laughing. Peggy Gerrish, and Rinda Curry and a girl who we called Gloucester could fire the rifle stood up, sat down, knelt down or laid down, no problem for them. The best part of this exercise was that the women didn't have to clean the weapons – we had to clean them. I would take a couple of mates on the range and fire the rifles until the barrels were hot, then pour eight pints of boiling water down each barrel, oil and pull them through until they were clean. This we used to enjoy.

A brigadier was coming to inspect (this happened every so often). There was always a guard of honour to give him the salute when he came into camp. The officers wanted to know within a few minutes as to what time he would enter the main gate so it was decided that we would do a little wireless scheme. One set would remain in the camp and one set would be somewhere near Croydon (in hiding). When the Brigadier passed the hide at Croydon, we would call in over the radio to let the guard know that his arrival was imminent. The RSM said that if we didn't get through we would all by up the creek without a paddle.

Thankfully our officer who had forgotten the batteries on one of our schemes was needed in the camp, so it was up to the rest of the team and we set up one radio behind a wall on the Croydon road. Our codeword was 'Blackbird'. When the Brigadier went by us we called: 'Hello Tare Uncle Baker Two Wun, Blackbird, Blackbird, I say again Blackbird, Over.' Back came the reply, 'Blackbird, Blackbird, Roger, Roger, over and out.' We then had to follow at a discreet distance. When the Brigadier had inspected the guard of honour, he went up the camp to the left while we went up to the right, put all the radio equipment back in the stores and parked the 15 cwt back on the vehicle park.

The Brigadier also went round the cookhouse during his visit along with the orderly officer and the ROS of the day.

'Any complaints?' asked the Brigadier.

'Yes sir, I've got a slug in my cabbage,' said Gnr Wright.

'Don't shout it out so loud, laddie, or everyone will want double meat rations,' said the Brigadier. At another table, a lad complained about his food being too hot with curry flavouring, so the Brigadier borrowed a spoon and tried it, then ate the lot saying he loved curry and had been in a regiment of Gurkha Rifles who ate hot curries on a regular basis.

Another lad asked the Brigadier if he could explain why we got a decent meal whenever top brass visited us. 'Take today for instance,' he said. 'Pineapple chunks and ice cream as desert, it's never happened before.'

'Don't know the answer to that one but don't you wish we would come more often?' He had answers to almost everything and asked one lad what his father did for a living. The lad said he was a civil servant.

The BSM said to the lad later on, 'That he was a fucking liar. Your father is not a civil servant.'

'Yes he is,' said the lad, 'but I couldn't tell the Brigadier that he's a fucking dustbinman.'

Who pissed in Granny's Oxo?

In every barrack room there was an iron pot-bellied stove. In the cold weather the room orderly would fill it up with coke during the day and at night we would fill it up before going to the NAAFI. Our stove had been filled up to within eight inches from the top, but when we came back from the NAAFI there was a terrible stench in the room. What is it? everyone was asking.

'Smells like piss,' said one lad, 'just as though someone has pissed on the fire.'

'How would you know that?' asked Weeks.

The lad said that he had worked in a garage, and that someone had pissed on their stove one day and he recognised the smell. There was a hissing noise coming from the stove, so someone lifted the lid and there was a tin can sat on top of the coke; whatever had been in it had now boiled away, but the stench hung about for days.

Lt Chappel asked what the smell was so we told him that we thought someone had played a joke on us with a tin full of piss. He said it was no joke and if the culprit was caught it would be a charge.

About a week later, one of the girls who had been charged for causing the disturbance at the guard room asked if there had been a funny smell in our barrack room.

'Yes,' we said.

'Revenge is sweet,' she said.

It seems that they had watched us go to the NAAFI, then had got someone to look out while they got into the barrack room and did the deed. We said no more about it but wondered where they had got the piss. Whenever Charlie Gladys saw the two girls after that he would shout to them, 'Who Pissed in Granny's Oxo?'

The Battery Office Clerk

The clerk in the battery office had been promoted at the same time as I had; since that occasion he had never done a guard duty of any kind, never came on a parade and never had to lose a night's sleep. I had many arguments with BSM Stamp about this and told him that as his clerk was a bombardier like I was, he should be doing his share of guard commander's duties; the sergeants were in agreement with me. If he had done a turn just now and again, it would have relieved the rest of the bombardiers who were covering sergeants' duties, but the BSM would have none of it, I suppose because he could get out of the office leaving his work to the clerk.

One night very late on, there was a knocking at the side of my hut, I opened the window and looked down. It was the battery office clerk's girlfriend. I asked her what was wrong and she said her boyfriend had collapsed on their way back from the pub. So I asked where he was, and if she thought he had had a heart attack. She said that he had not had any heart attack but was roaring drunk when he passed out and was now laid in the woods behind the joiner's shop (Tomlinson's hideout). 'Can you get some help to bring him back to the billet?' she asked. I got two of the lads to come with me with torches, and we followed her to where he was. It was a bitterly cold night and he was stark naked lying in a pool of water.

I asked her where his clothes were, and she said he had taken them off as he was walking, leaving them scattered along the path from the main road. Whey had he taken them off on such a cold night? She said that he was feeling frisky and was going to have a jump (as she put it). We staggered back to the billets with him between us, having first collected his clothes and giving them to her to carry. We carried him in, put him on his bed and moved it near to the stove, whereupon she banged on the side of the hut and one of the lads went back out to collect his clothes from her. She asked him if he would give her one.

'One what?' asked the lad.

'A good shagging,' she said. 'Just because he's collapsed doesn't mean I have to go without.'

He called us to go outside. 'What do you think she said to me?' he asked.

'Don't know,' we said.

He said, 'She has asked me to shag her.'

'Well go on if you want to,' we said.

'I wouldn't shag her with his prick,' he said, pointing to the other lad. The other lad said, 'No, and I wouldn't lend it to you.'

'You're a pair of rotten bastards,' she told them. 'What about you?' she asked, looking at me.

'No thank you,' I said, 'go back to your quarters.'

'And you're a rotten spoilsporting bastard,' she said.

About a week later we were chatting in the X Troop barrack room; the talk as usual was SEX. How many women have you been with? they were asking each other. One lad said that he had been lucky one night about a week before and had his first jump ever. Of course there were chants of 'Fucking liar' and many other obscene expressions. But he went on to relate, as he was on prowler guard he had been approached by the girlfriend of the battery clerk (naming her). She told him that she was going to 'Vamp him.' 'What's that?' he had asked her. She said she was going to shag him, so he said to her that he had never done it before; she told him that it would be his first lesson. He said that he was highly delighted and was like a dog with ten tails (wagging them all). He said that when the marching relief had come to change him over, both the marching relief and the new sentry had had a go, and that he was waiting for his next lesson. The chorus of voices shouted again 'Fucking liar.' I was able to confirm that his story could possibly be true.

Chapter XXVIII

My Very Last Guard Duty – Getting near to Demob

I WAS DOING MY LAST GUARD MOUNTING DUTY and had called out to the lads to inspect them before going down to where the orderly officer would inspect us, lining them up on the wide footpath between the men's and women's billets. A few of the windows on the women's side came open – some of the women just wanted to watch the guard mounting, some wanted to 'Take the Piss'. There were mocking calls from some of the women as I gave orders. 'Playing soldiers again, are we?' they chanted. Then the windows of our barrack rooms opened and a stirrup pump started squirting off to one side of us, right into the window of the women's quarters. Then all hell broke loose, women were running outside with fire buckets full of water and throwing them into the windows of the men's quarters. The guard were caught in the middle – we got away but not before we were soaked.

There was no way that guard mounting could be held up. When the ROS came to inspect us ready for the orderly officer, he nearly choked, didn't bother to inspect, but just had us wait for the orderly officer. In the meantime there was a full-scale water battle going on at the billets. Many others had joined in; men were filling baths with cold water then dragging the WRACs inside and immersing them in the baths; there were also indecent assaults going on in the pretence of play fighting. Women were being held under the showers (we heard about it later). The orderly officer did his nut and we had to go and get changed leaving the RPs to hold the fort. No one would admit who started it off. Everyone in the two lots of billets were confined to barracks for seven days ... all except the guard.

Mick Ayres had been made up to lance bombardier, and it had been decided that as I was getting near to demob he would take over the inventory of X Troop barrack room. At last I was free from the responsibility of having government stores on my signature. Some time later a new intake was coming in, so all our intake who were going out were moved into marquees which were pitched at the top end of the assault course. Mick and his lot were moved into our billets and women were moved into their billets.

The WRAC Corporal who had signed over the barracks room from Mick had checked the inventory and found she had a bed missing. CSM Mallard had been told about the missing bed and wanted to know where it was. As I was walking down the camp between the huts I was stopped by the CSM who told me that if I saw Lance Bombardier Ayres I should tell him that he was wanted by her. Passing by one of the lecture rooms I saw Mick sat in the corner at the back of the lecture room near to a broken window. Without thinking I tapped on the glass and when Mick looked up I told him that CSM Mallard wanted to see him, so Mick asked the officer who was taking the lecture if he could be excused because the CSM wanted to see him. The officer then asked Mick how he knew that the CSM wanted to see him, so Mick told him that I had just passed the window and told him. The officer then told Mick that when he saw me he should tell me that he wanted to see me.

Mick was wandering round looking for the CSM and saw me coming back up the camp; he told me the officer wanted to see me and that he wasn't very pleased about the way I had informed him that he was wanted. CSM Mallard then came into view, and proceeded to give Mick a verbal earbashing about the missing bed, which of course he knew nothing about – some months earlier I had refused to sign an inventory because it didn't tally with the amount of beds in the room and another inventory had been made out … I had got Mick to sign that same one … someone must have got hold of the wrong one when Mick handed over to the WRAC Corporal. The CSM went on that her corporal was not going to pay for a missing bed, so I explained all about it and said that the old inventory should have been thrown away. I was told most politely to fuck off and mind my own business.

But Mick was adamant and asked if she thought he had stolen a bed to start his own hospital (he didn't often swear). It was resolved eventually when the proper inventory was found so that no one had to pay for a bed, but what a mystery.

I went to see the officer who I had offended. What a bollocking I got! He said I should have entered the room and asked his permission to excuse Mick. He was right, of course I should, but seeing Mick there I didn't think. He was going to charge me although as a bombardier I would have only got admonished. And as was pointed out to him when he reported me to the BSM, what would he put on the charge sheet?

> 22393919 Bombardier Barraclough. To the prejudice of Good Order and Military Discipline in that you did on the said date at Hobbs Barracks Lingfield speak through a broken window.

The BSM told him that he would give me a good bollocking, but he didn't because, as he said, he owed me a favour.

Chapter XXIX

The Last Few Days at Hobbs

WE NOW DIDN'T HAVE MUCH TO DO so one of the officers decided on a map reading scheme. He would go all over Lingfield/East Grinstead and surrounding areas and make arrangements for checking points. We were sent out in twos, with a map and compass. What we had to do was find our way around the course he set, calling in at the arranged check points i.e. Station Master at East Grinstead who would sign our list to prove we had been; Post Office at Forest Row who would sign etc. It was also a test of initiative – get lifts if you could and see who got back quickest.

Ron Jones (Standish, Wigan) went along with me; on the last leg of our journey we thumbed a lift when a Rover car pulled up with a very old lady driver. We got in the back imagining that the old man in front was her husband. They were both interested in what we were doing, and asked many questions about the National Serviceman's lot. Suddenly a car came out from a side road, our driver had to brake hard and probably forgetting that we were in the back, both she and the man shouted in very posh voices, 'Fucking stupid bastard', also giving the other driver a two-fingered gesture. They then apologised to us, saying that we had probably never heard a woman use bad language before. 'Don't you believe it,' we said. 'Just come and listen to some of the WRAC at Hobbs Barracks.'

The day after the map exercise the officer decided to have a route march – 5 miles out of camp and 5 miles back with a lorry sent out for anyone who fell by the wayside. Two of the women officers decided they would tag along. 'Good exercise,' they said.

In a narrow country lane we got some cars behind us who had to wait for an opportunity to overtake us. We always marched facing the oncoming traffic and also afforded the courtesy to the motorists to have a look out and wave them on when it was clear for them to go. One chap had been waiting a short while to get past. When he was waved on, and not knowing there were women officers there, he shouted as he passed, 'Why don't you keep in your barracks, you fucking road hogs?' Sgt Wingate said if he had stopped he would have kicked his goolies up into his mouth.

98

German 88mm, Muckleburgh Collection, Weybourne, Norfolk.

British 3.7 Field and Ack-Ack. Botany Bay, Chorley, Lancashire.
[Note the similarity between the two guns above].

About a mile further on we came across the same car which had skidded into a hedge, his front wheels were in the ditch. 'Can you men push me out of here?' the man said to the officer. He was going to say yes, because being at the front he hadn't heard the man shout at us, but one of the women officers came up from the rear. 'No,' she said, 'why don't you keep to the road you fucking hedgehog?'

Back at the camp we were told that we had to wash our feet, then lay on our beds and stick our feet over the bottom rail as a medical orderly came to examine them for blisters. We were all stretched out with feet over the edge when in came this chap with a bag over his shoulder (it was the type of bag used by paper boys). He didn't say much but seemed to be looking at our feet as he walked up by our beds. There was the usual banter going on with some of the lads saying how they fancied the women officers who had been with us. Then Charlie started on the chap with the bag. 'Have you ever had a good jump, Snake?' he asked the man. Many more lads were coming out with crude remarks, some insinuating that the chap was a poof.

'What have you got in the sack?' asked one lad. 'Is it ointment and bandages for our feet?'

'No,' said the man, 'I have got Bibles in the bag, but it seems to me that you lot belong in Sodom and Gomorrah.'

'Where's that?' shouted someone as the chap beat a hasty retreat.

In came the medical orderly. 'Oh!' he said, 'I see you lot have had the local Methodist minister to see you.'

The following night we had a bit of a booze-up in the NAAFI to celebrate our leaving the Army next morning.

Geordie Raffles gave us a very good recital on the piano, and many other lads who could play instruments also joined in as we had a good sing-song.

You'll never go to Heaven on roller skates
Because you'll never pass those pearly gates.
You'll never go to Heaven on a 3.7, the Lord don't
allow no guns in Heaven.
I ain't going to grieve my Lord no more.

The girls were singing this with many verses while the lads were singing:

They say that Hobbs Barracks is a very nice place
but the organisations a fucking disgrace.
There's sergeants and corporals and officers too
with their hands in their pockets and fuck all to do.
They stand on the square and they bawl and they shout
about things that they know fuck all about.
So come down to Hobbs Barracks and there you will see
the mountains of bullshit that sweep down to the sea.

Sung to the tune of 'Mountains of Mourne'.

The first thing we pray for we pray for our king
for O what a good King to us he had been.
And when we win one war may we win another ten,
We'll kill the fucking enemy was the soldiers' amen.
The next thing we pray for we pray for some beer,
O if we had some it would make us feel queer.
When we have had one pint may we have another ten,
We could drink a fucking brewery was the soldiers' amen.

The last thing we pray for we pray for the wife,
May she be happy for the rest of her life.
When she had had one child may she have another ten,
May she have a fucking regiment was the soldiers' amen.

How many of us would be fit to travel home?

Captain Chappel, as he now was, came and asked me if I would sign on and be promoted to sergeant. 'Yes,' I said, 'Providing I can get posted somewhere else.'

'Not very likely,' he said.

We left the Army on 31 July 1952.

Oh! What will the girls of Lingfield say
When the Artillery gunners march away?
Come back you bastards we'll make you pay
For leaving us all in the family way.

Then started our three and a half years on the Army Emergency Reserve.

Sayings of Different NCOs

'Am I hurting you, lad?' 'No sir.' 'Well I fucking well should be, I'm standing on your hair. Get it cut.' (Sgt Bayliss)

'If you cleaned you badge this morning, my prick is a fucking screwdriver.' (Sgt Eyles)

'Did you shave this morning?' 'Yes sir.' 'Well if you fucking shaved this morning I'm Adolph Hitler's dog.' (Sgt Brittain)

Every NCO had his own: (BSM Stamp) My fucking cock's a kipper. My knob's a bloater. I'll stick my boot up your arse to the third lacehole.

Dear Mother, life in the Army is a bastard. Dear Son, so are you but don't tell your father. (Sgt Russell)

Dear Mother, sell the pig and buy me out of the Army. (Sgt Wingate)

How is you memory after nearly fifty years?